You Can't Save Your Way to Wealth

How YOU can build generational wealth through real estate, take care of your immediate family and fund your retirement, even if you're an immigrant, have no savings and have bad credit.

To Sumantha

Zeb Tsikira

Zeb Tsikira and Colleen Tsikira

Visit the author's website at https://www.thetsikiras.com
ebook ISBN: 978-1-7773851-1-8
Softcover ISBN: 978-1-7773851-2-5

Disclaimer:

While we make every effort to ensure that we accurately represent all the strategies and methods inside this book, our website, Facebook group and other supporting documents and their potential for income. It should be noted that earnings and income statements made by the authors are examples and estimates only of what we think you can possibly earn. There is no guarantee that you will make any level of income and you accept the risk that the success, earnings and income statements differ by individual.

As with any business, your results may vary, and will be based on your individual capacity, business experience, expertise, and level of desire. There are no guarantees concerning the level of success you may experience. The stories, testimonials and examples used are exceptional results, which do not apply to the average person, and are not intended to represent or guarantee that anyone will achieve the same or similar results. Each individual's success depends on his, her or their background, dedication, desire and motivation.

There is no assurance that examples of past earnings can be duplicated in the future. We cannot guarantee your future results and/or success. There are some unknown risks in business that we cannot foresee which could reduce the results you experience. We are not responsible for your actions.

The use of our information, products and services should be based on your own due diligence and you agree that the authors are not liable for any success or failure of your business that is directly or indirectly related to the purchase and use of the information, products and services shared inside this book.

Table of Contents

Preface

Before you begin, please know this is not your typical book about money, wealth, real estate, and financial freedom. This book is meant to shift your thinking about how YOU can build generational wealth through real estate, take care of your immediate family and fund your retirement, even if you're an immigrant, have no savings and have bad credit.

We wanted to write this book because we are passionate about helping people, especially immigrants, become financially free. We know what it feels like to embark on something new, without support, feeling alone, without all the knowledge, and then make all the mistakes. We also know how it feels to be on the other side now reaping the fruits of our labour and feeling great about the future for our children and family.

Our intention with this book is to give people like you the inspiration and foundation to start your journey to grow generational wealth. We want to share how to be smart with your money, leverage other people's money to grow your investments, turn your home into an income generating asset, instead of a liability, and to use the golden handcuffs of your job to jumpstart your real estate investment portfolio. You don't have to stay stuck where you are. We believe in you!

We know you may already be wondering if this is possible for you. We've seen it time and time again. You don't have to come from money, have a college education, or be financially savvy right now, but you do need the desire and the willingness to learn. You can do, have and become anything you desire. It's totally available for you and you can do this! This is your chance to change the trajectory of your life and that of future generations.

To support you, we've also included links and downloads to expand your learning. Make sure you take advantage of the extra video links and templates we share so you don't have to create them yourself. We would also love for you to join us in our Facebook community called 16WeekInvestor here: https://www.facebook.com/groups/16weekinvestor/ .

We have students and investors from all around the world who are looking to start or grow their existing portfolio. And we always say you learn more and achieve more with other like-minded people in your circle.

We consider ourselves to be very straightforward in our approach. We want to teach you from the lens of our experience over the last ten years. We believe you can avoid mistakes and shortcut your learning by absorbing lessons from others who have gone before you – that's exactly what we've done when we have hired mentors and coaches to help us.

We also know many immigrants will read this book and English may not be their first language so we made sure to keep things simple. While there are potentially some new financial, real estate or mortgage words, we do our best to define them within the book so you can read and feel confident with your next steps.

In truth, sometimes it really did feel like the odds were stacked against us. That's why we want to be transparent with our stories and share the behind the scenes reality. We've seen too many books that only share the upside of real estate investing and we felt that was a big disservice. You'll end up misguided and misinformed. So we wanted to go deeper with the stories in this book. They are real stories and based on our own lives, along with the experiences of our clients and friends. We wanted to share the times where it felt like things weren't working out. It's not to scare you off. It's to make sure you know the truth. We got through it and we know you can too.

As long as you are always learning and growing, everything is a lesson and everything can be turned into a win. You'll hear about some of the properties we purchased that turned out really well and other properties that helped us learn great lessons. We hope that by sharing them, you can shortcut your learning curve and be encouraged to start your journey to financial freedom with us.

This book really is three books in one. We know time is priceless so we refrained from writing a 100,000 word book and instead wrote a book where you could learn quickly. We packed this book with what we wished we had known when we started. Each part could stand on its own, but together it gives you a great strategy.

Part 1: Financial Literacy is where we make sure you understand the basics of money and money management.

Part 2: Your Mortgage Helper is where we share how to turn your first home into an income generating property

Part 3: Real Estate Investing 101 is where we give you the foundational pieces to become successful in real estate investing so you can grow your wealth and realize financial freedom.

Please feel free to connect with us:

Youtube: http://bit.ly/tsikirasyt

Website: www.thetsikiras.com
www.16weekinvestor.com (Our course)

Social Media: www.facebook.com/ZebTsikira/
www.facebook.com/thetsikiras/
www.instagram.com/thetsikiras/

Community:
          www.facebook.com/groups/16weekinvestor/

Introduction

When people meet us, they see a couple who have a sizable and impressive real estate portfolio. They also see a couple who have opened more than 20 successful and a few failed businesses over the last 10 years leading them to ask us for business and real estate investing advice. We have been interviewed on numerous podcasts and shows expanding our reach and making an impacting. We have been able to help our students from all around the world start their real estate investment portfolios using what we have learned over the years. A lot of times, people think that things just fell together perfectly for us, which is far from the truth as we didn't just start out that way.

While most people notice how well we work together and how we travel with our children, what they don't fully grasp is that we didn't always have the answers. We didn't have piles of money laying around to invest in real estate, we didn't inherit anything and we didn't always have family members cheering us on.

In fact, it was somewhat the opposite. We started out as two average blue collar employees with a goal of breaking generational curses of poverty and feeling like we were not enough.
I remember growing up and being told no, "We can't afford it" and developing a feeling that I never wanted my kids to experience.

What we now teach our students to ask instead is, "What are you willing to do or give up for it?" This develops a sense of responsibility and feeling like a part of the solution than a cause of the problem.

From humble beginnings of just knowing we could achieve something we had only read about in books, seen on TV and witnessed in seminars, we were ready to put in the work. What we did have was dedication, a great work ethic and having each other to stay focused.

Then came the day when we learned that we can't save our way to wealth. After saving $12,000, in what felt like forever, we took a look at our statement and were gutted to notice the nanoscopic interest we had earned from leaving our money in the bank. We did however have a better plan. We had been working three jobs each. Colleen was an administrative assistant at a local accounting firm, worked at a coffee shop and hotel front desk. Zeb worked as a teller, was a driving instructor and worked overnight as a security guard. After a long and hard three months, we had saved the money we needed for a down payment. We were so excited and proud to walk up to the bank with $12,000 in hand and ready to buy our first home.

We opened those double glass doors to the bank with smiles on our faces, expecting to walk out with financing. Instead, the bank told us our credit was unsatisfactory, showed us all the flaws, and told us that we didn't qualify. Again, we were gutted! We didn't know that our credit card debts of $45,000 combined were a huge deterrent to a bank lending us on a mortgage. As new immigrants we didn't know how the credit system worked and, unfortunately, this was our crash course on what it meant to receive a credit card.

With plan A out the window and a flop, we went home with a gallon of ice cream between us discussing what we would do with the money now. Would we take a vacation? We contemplated blowing it on something fun but, we knew it would only be temporary. By the time we got to the bottom of that ice cream container, we were that much more committed to making our dream of purchasing properties and becoming financially free come true. We knew we had to keep the promise we made to ourselves and concentrate only on our end goal.

Both of us had been highly influenced by Robert Kiyosaki and his Cash Flow game. We knew that we didn't want to be in the "rat race" forever and we also knew that working all these jobs for the rest of our lives would get us nowhere, with nothing to show at the end of our lives.

As Bernie Sanders once said, "The main problem of America is that you're seeing people working all over this country doing two jobs, they're working three jobs, and they're getting nowhere in a hurry. They're working hard. They can't afford to send their kids to college in many instances. They can't afford child care for their little babies. They're worried to death about retirement."
This resonated with us and as somewhat still newlyweds looking to our future, we desired something better.

Colleen's parents had always encouraged us to open our own business after Zeb had received multiple requests for private driving lessons outside of his normal work. The timing was perfect when Zeb was laid off. So instead of buying our first house, we used that $12,000 to invest in a new business and purchase our first vehicle which was a 2009 Ford Focus. We had it fixed along to regulatory specifications and went on our way. The next step was to get our business license and insurance. We made the required documentation and the wheels of progress were in motion. During the lunch hour of our regular jobs, we would sometimes teach people how to drive. Then after work, Zeb would instruct from 5:00 pm to 9:00 pm and then go to his overnight security job. On the weekends, we would load up on all the driving we could squeeze in and run our business.

A year later, on November 16, 2012, the doors of the bank welcomed us in a different way. We had saved up $30,000 by this time and were swiftly approved for a home. We were able to subsidize our rent and start saving after years of house hacking where we started by sharing a 2 bedroom apartment with 4 others. At that time we had 2 roommates in the living area, then we graduated to renting out a single room in the only apartment available in town, which is a story for another day but just know that this taught us the importance of curb appeal. We had fixed our credit and our new condo was perfect, a two-bedroom villa with a den. At that point we felt we had achieved success and could do without the roommates. One evening during a family game night, Colleen brought out a game she had played in college for us to try. This was the Cashflow Game. Needless to say, the next day our condo was on the market and the journey to our investing success was launched. Four years later, on October 2, 2016, Colleen celebrated by quitting her job. She finally felt free and happy. All those days trading time for money was draining and no matter how hard we both worked, we knew we couldn't save our way to wealth. It was just too much and we're so thankful that those jobs were temporary.

As you might imagine, around this time our two children were born, Ethan and Zoe, in 2015 and 2017 respectively. To say that becoming parents changed our perspective is an understatement. While we are extremely passionate about real estate, we are even more passionate about giving our children the life that we envisioned. We want to have the ability to do whatever we want with them, whenever we want. Gone are the days of needing to request time off, only to be denied, and now we get to create generational wealth while we do it.

Now, we are so excited to share that we are property millionaires and currently financially free! It only took three years for us to achieve financial freedom through real estate investing and in the process, we created a system that we can confidently teach our students.

Not only was Colleen able to quit her full time job, but Zeb purchased his dream car, The Range Rover Sport Supercharged. We now spend our days growing our businesses, travelling the world and nurturing our purpose.

None of these things would've been possible if we hadn't committed to our vision and pushed through our fears (we promise you a lot of them came up). We took the necessary steps towards investing not just in real estate, but in ourselves, even when it was scary. See, real estate isn't the best investment you can make -- the best investment you can make is in yourself.

Of course, we know that real estate investing can be a little daunting or even intimidating because there seems to be so much to learn. It may even seem like the industry is uncertain or changes often, but what we learned was to keep our eyes on our vision, follow our instincts, and get a mentor. We allowed ourselves to make mistakes and were armed with research to make the best decisions ... and it worked.

You may be asking yourself why we wanted to write this book and why now? Well, the truth is, we want to help others achieve financial freedom. There's a point in many successful people's lives where they've come so far and the missing piece to the puzzle is giving back and helping others achieve the same. Wealth and abundance is available for everyone. Whatever your dream is, we trust you can achieve it by believing in yourself and leveraging the power of real estate investing.

And that's why it's now our honour and blessing to be able to share our life experiences and lessons with people just like you. We truly believe that people out there need to learn about real estate and find the freedom in their lives that we found for ours.

Our first "why" is our beautiful children. We've worked hard to create a legacy for them and future generations whom we may never even meet. There comes a time when man perishes but we hope our stories and lessons live on and that's why our next "why" is our students. We never know what the future holds, but we know that anyone who wants to achieve their vision of becoming financially free can do it through real estate investing and we'd love for you to join us in the impact we're creating.

So we are documenting our journey through this book and the houses that we buy on YouTube (http://bit.ly/tsikirasyt), Facebook (www.facebook.com/thetsikiras/) and Instagram (https://www.instagram.com/thetsikiras/) to show that you can do this too – the only thing you need to do right now is to choose financial freedom for your life. It's our mission to share the opportunity that's available to you, if you want to go on a similar journey.

Part 1:
Financial
Literacy

Chapter 1

The Shift Needed in

"The American Dream"

THE TRUTH ABOUT THE AMERICAN DREAM

"A dream doesn't become reality through magic; it takes sweat, determination and hard work."
— COLIN POWELL

We truly believe immigrants have a head start when it comes to mindset and determination. Nobody is more dedicated and committed to working hard, getting a good job, paying their bills, supporting their family and sending money back home. According to Stats Canada, in 2017: (2)

- 37% of Canadian residents born in countries eligible for Official Development Assistance sent money abroad to relatives or friends. Men (38%) remitted slightly more than women (36%).
- Canadian residents born in ODA-eligible countries remitted $5.2 billion in 2017. This amount was unevenly distributed between men and women
- Remitters sent $2,855 yearly on average.
- The average amount remitted in 2017 ranged from $1,825 for remitters born in the Americas to $4,755 for those born in Eastern Asia.

- At the country level, the Philippines, India, the United States, China and Pakistan were the top five destinations of remittances from Canada.

A study undertaken by Statistics Canada in 2017, revealed that Filipino residents in Canada made the highest number of international remittances than any other group. A whopping $1.2 billion was transferred to friends and family according to the data recorded. The agency further highlighted that Filipino women made up a very large proportion of immigrants admitted to Canada under the live-in care program in 2017. According to data from the 2016 census, Filipino-Canadians were the fourth largest visible minority group in the country.

Further research and study by Statistics Canada revealed that the majority of the funds were sent to help in the upkeep of family members back home. According to the data, 59% of the remittances were to help pay for food, housing, utilities, electricity and heat while 43% of the respondents said the money was for medical costs. 35% of the respondents said they sent the money as a gift, which is a frequent occurrence among those from high-income countries.

As immigrants ourselves, we know that there's a strong sense of responsibility regarding sending money home and taking care of other people. What if instead of working so hard, we could share how you can work smarter? What if you could achieve as much or more without working as hard as you are today?

From our experience, we've seen immigrants working two, three jobs or more! One job covers living expenses here and the second is for family support back home. The third job serves as the fun or investment fund for things like a road trip, car, vacations or buying a home or other things. While we commend this family loyalty, it's time to shift that thinking because you can invest your money instead to get way ahead.

Gary Vaynerchuk says, "I think being born in Belarus, coming here with nothing, my parents working every minute - that instilled a huge competitive advantage, a chip on my shoulder, a work ethic. Immigrants win a lot and they win a lot because of a couple core things."
Now, a big part of living in the land of milk and honey is believing you can do it and the opportunity is available to you. You aren't stuck where you are today, you're not stuck where your parents or grandparents may have been stuck. There's no such thing as, "This is the way it's always been for my family for generations." You can make a different choice and create the life you've always wanted, thereby changing the lives of future generations.

Growing up in Zimbabwe as a family of 9, we didn't have much. I remember only getting new shoes and clothes on Christmas day. One memory that is ingrained in my mind is of my 2 younger brothers and me sitting on the living room floor trying to figure out whose "Payday" it was. Our parents were part of reciprocal "lending" clubs also known as stokvels.

A stokvel is a popular savings club among group members with a set target of contributions. The members would agree on the amount which everyone would contribute and then create a roster to decide who gets the first collection. The recipients would then rotate until every contributing member had received their share. If a group had five members, for instance, and they agreed on contributions of $100 each per month, that meant Member 1 would get $500 at the end of the month. The following month Member 2 would be the recipient of the pooled funds and so on until each member had received.

Once or twice a month for our morning breakfast, we would have two to three slices of bread and tea each. For growing boys in their teens, this usually wasn't enough. We decided to use the stokvels idea but instead of money, our currency would be bread!
Later on, we realized that we could apply the same principles from the stokvel concept in our real estate investing journey. We created a platform to connect with like-minded and eager investors who are interested in pooling financial resources together to purchase real estate. Investing as a group makes property ownership accessible to more people. It also opens up exciting prospects such as purchasing residential properties as well as land to develop for commercial or industrial purposes.

When you read this book, we want to challenge you to step out of your normal circle, just like we did! As you read on, you might be excited or inspired by some information and feel compelled to share your new-found knowledge. It is important to be mindful that not everyone will catch on to your fire and share your enthusiasm. People are wired differently like that so do not despair when some seem skeptical about it. Remember, success wasn't built in comfort zones and this is where our community will be your support system. We share the analogy of building a home to our students as follows: the more you give your bricks away, the harder it will be to complete your house. Once you are standing on a solid foundation, you may then share what you have learned because you are being called to transform your entire community.

Sometimes we may give examples using numbers that sound bigger than what you will start with but don't let that scare you. We definitely have not forgotten what it was like to have nothing saved or to be struggling to pay the rent. We started from scratch, just like many of our students, and worked our way from our first investment property (and all the mistakes we made with it) to now owning almost a hundred doors.

Remember that everyone starts somewhere. Every real estate investor who now owns millions of dollars in real estate started with just one. Like we mentioned, many immigrants consider themselves to have won the jackpot just by getting here, getting a good job, and making good money to support their family. Don't forget that the other part of the dream is to one day, sooner rather than later, be able to retire without any financial worries.

If your current dream is to go back home with $50,000 saved, your dream is much like our parents. But we want to challenge you to dream bigger. It's not just about having a good job and being content with a nice white picket-fence house. We know you've already won by just making it here from your country, but there's an even bigger opportunity that's fully available to you, so don't miss out by keeping your dream too small.

Know that there will be people who don't believe you can do it. There might be days when that person is you, but don't let anyone try to impose their views on you. After all, many people didn't think that Thomas Edison could make the light bulb; and probably thought he was crazy. See what happened with his dedication? Take time to find a community that believes in the same thing you do. Surround yourself with thought leaders. You will be encouraged when you realize that you are not the odd crazy one determined to achieve financial freedom. Other like-minded people in the community become your support in shared goals.

Instead, surround yourself with people who want to achieve the same thing. Because we know how important that is, we've created a Facebook community called "16WeekInvestor" where you could come in and see other people who are succeeding, who also understand where you are and what you're working to achieve. We also share tools and tips in there on how to make those moves.

THE SHIFT NEEDED

We were talking to a student of ours who was so set on buying a house back home, *"So now when I go back home, I'm not staying at my parent's house. We're going to purchase a three- bedroom house. It's going to be spacious and we're going to pay cash for it."*

Using this example, let's dive in a little more. Let's say it's going to cost $100,000 for this house. You may visit and stay in this house two months out of a year. What's going to happen to the house when you're away? You'll need to find somebody who will stay and watch it. So now you're paying someone to watch your house sit or have family stay for free. There are wear and tear and maintenance costs too. Then there's all the furniture you have to buy. Most people don't consider all of this and our student was the same way.

What if instead you take that same hundred thousand to use as a down payment to buy a house? Twenty percent down as an investor gets you a house at $500,000 with the cash flow of $1,000 every month. You could take that $12,000 at the end of the year and rent a beautiful Airbnb for two months and now you're living like a king/queen. The house back home is not even an asset -- it's a liability that's draining and costing you money. Instead, if you buy a property that generates income, now you have a $12,000 a year budget to go have a luxurious vacation back home.

I think sometimes, as immigrants, we put ourselves under so much pressure to show that we have made it. It's totally unnecessary to prove ourselves so much. In real estate investing, we are showing our students how to buy properties for zero down. Because they are so proud they've raised five percent, they want to use that money as a downpayment, even if it's not needed. If you can leverage a zero down property, you can save that money for a deal where it's necessary. Don't just use the money to prove you have it -- it's not a competition.

For some investors starting out, $100,000 is unimaginable. Let's explore an example with a little less. What if you had $20,000. What would the options look like then? Consider if you could syndicate (join) or collaborate with other like-minded people using your $20,000 instead of buying one house or waiting to save up for a bigger down payment. However with 20 of us, each with $20,000, we could start looking at bigger investments like an apartment building. All of a sudden, what you may have thought would take a long time or never happen, becomes a reality. Maybe you've never thought about this possibility before but this is how a different mindset shift happens. When you decide to work together in collaborations such as these, you eliminate the competition and instead change everyone's life.

As an overview, there are four shifts in mindset that are foundational to your financial freedom.

1. Shift your mindset from being happy with two or more endless jobs to support family, to one job for living and the second for investing.
2. If you're going to buy a house, buy one where you can get help paying your mortgage. We call this a mortgage helper and will discuss it in full detail in Part 2.
3. If you can only raise $20,000, instead of keeping it in the bank where it will take a long time to double; check out the Rule of 72 and use that money to invest in a cash flowing asset. You can do this with a single property or through collaboration.

4. Lastly, make the bank your business partner. If you could leverage that relationship, you could potentially get into deals you normally couldn't afford, including apartment buildings.

If you didn't come from a rich family, then a rich family must come from you. Say to yourself, "If it is to be, then it's up to me!" One generation down, our kids will get to say that my parents were part of this initiative. This has far-reaching implications because when we purchase real estate we're building communities. This is how we create influence and change the system by controlling schooling and then the education system. Now we can change the financial literacy problem through our financial power. See how this trickles down to more than just real estate? We are repairing our communities which build future business leaders in every industry.

Chapter 2

Gather your BRICK

We like to talk about the steps to financial literacy with the term BRICK. Bricks are foundational in building a house and foundational to building financial freedom. Think about collecting BRICKs for your house. You can't give away BRICKs before your house is built -- you need to keep your BRICKs so your house can be fully built. To get to the point where you can start to think about giving away extra BRICKs or sending them home, you need to invest so your money can work for you to multiply the BRICKs you have. Then support your community.

As an example, you can invest to get cash flow through buying properties. Then you can build a home where you live instead of sending your income back home. You may need to have a heart-to-heart conversation with those you love so they understand what you're doing. Remember, you're building your financial freedom so never ask for permission to do this. Even if they don't understand, you'll be able to help them even more in the future if you build this base. They'll see the benefit later because when you have an asset (your home or homes) that produces cash flow as income, you can send as many excess BRICKs to support your family, but you have to gather your own BRICKs first.

Here's what each letter of BRICK stands for:

BANK savings

It's not about how much you make, it's about how much you keep. The truth is you can't save your way to wealth. A lot of people think if you make $80,000 a year, you're rich, or if you've hit 6-figures, you've made it, but you're not keeping all of it. Most people keep almost nothing from their income. In fact, the average rate of savings for Canadians is 1.7%, which means that those earning $50,000 a year are only saving $850. In 40 years, assuming 6% returns and 2% inflation, you would have just over $137,000 to fund your retirement, which isn't enough.[5] When we take a look at the median overall savings of American households, it's currently only $4,830 and 31 percent say they can't save anything.

- 41.13% of those aged 18-24 have no savings.
- 50% of those aged 25-34 have no savings.
- 40.91% of those aged 35-44 have no savings.
- 54.29% of those aged 45-54 have no savings.
- 40.24% of those aged 55-64 have no savings.

What's even more concerning is:
- 22 percent of Americans have less than $5,000 in retirement savings
- 46 percent expect to keep working after the age of 65.

In an emergency,
- 23 percent say they can't afford to spend $100.[1]

The problem is most people wait until their children are 18, while they're in college or graduating from college, to have a conversation about money and financial literacy. Additionally, most people are ill-equipped to have the conversation in the first place because they weren't taught proper financial literacy either. Who knows what kind of misinformation is being handed down from generation to generation? One of our friend's nephews even thought that if a bank was located inside a grocery store, it wasn't a "real" bank. There are way too many people who are blind about how to manage their money.

"Those who don't manage their money will always work for those who do." ~ Dave Ramsey

Now, please don't get us wrong. We are not suggesting that you love money above anything else. What we are hoping to help you accomplish is to create the freedom of having your money work for you. Many of us were taught to follow a specific path. In some homes, you are either a doctor, a lawyer or a failure. While this can be great for some people, it doesn't work for many others. They were meant for other things, like being an entrepreneur or real estate investor. If this is you, knowing how to get your money to work for you will free up your time and allow you to do whatever your heart desires.

It seems like schools leave it up to fate that we will learn financial literacy instead of teaching it. Had we been taught about money in school, we would have known better, done better, and saved ourselves some pain. Right now we're not using all of our education. Instead, we're leaning mostly on our specialized financial knowledge in order to develop what we have now and that's something that we had to learn outside of school. We both didn't even sit down to learn how to balance a checkbook until later in life, so that's why we think it's so important to educate people as early as possible.

We believe that the best time to share the knowledge of money starts at a young age. Our kids are currently five and three and we started talking to them about money as soon as we felt they could understand simple financial concepts. In many ways, teaching your children how to manage their money is the most important gift you can give them. We can't emphasize enough that financial literacy needs to start at home. Too often parents think that it's their responsibility to pay the bills and shield the kids from anything that has to do with the bills. Perhaps they think the kids are too young or maybe they were stressed out about money in their childhood and don't want their children to go through the same emotions. The problem is that those kids grow up not knowing about finances and, remember, school isn't teaching them either. In the end, they're thrust into adulthood without the proper knowledge to succeed at the money game. Now you've unwittingly perpetrated a generational curse. The way out of this is to start learning now, fill in the gaps in your financial literacy, and start talking to your children as early as possible. Then when they need to talk to a bank, they will know if that bank will lend them money before they even ask.

Let's start with the habit of saving. A lot of people just don't have a saving habit. After all, how could we when we are collectively sending over $5.2 billion a year back home. Savings is something that can be learned from a young age. Currently, we're teaching our kids to save 50 percent of their income. Whether it's money that came as a birthday gift or a gift card, they'll save 50 percent of that gift and they get to spend the other 50 percent. They usually forget most of the time because they're not at an age where they remember, but this is cultivating habits at an early stage. When you teach your kids to start saving, that's something that will come easy to them at an older age. It's much easier than trying to break a bad habit.

Unfortunately, a lot of immigrants are spenders. If they're not sending money home, they feel the need to reward themselves for their hard work. They may feel like they deserve to walk around with a Louis Vuitton bag. If you've ever noticed, the minority population are the biggest consumers of luxury and name brand items because they show status. They somehow say that we've made it.

We are so focused on creating an image that we forget that, at the end of the day, we need to care more about what's coming into our wallets and how much money we are saving and investing for our futures.

So the first thing is to focus on the mindset of saving. Then start saving so it becomes an easy, automatic habit. Then give it a goal. A goal of $10,000 is a great start. You can also do it as a percentage and use 20-50 percent of your income as a guideline.

If your goal is to use money to buy a property, first determine the price of the income property you're trying to purchase. That calculation will tell you how much money you need depending on if you're putting five percent or twenty percent down. You will need at least five percent for your primary residence and a minimum of twenty percent for an investment property. You can target five percent to start if you're not sure.

When you start saving, if it hasn't been a habit, the most common struggle is instant gratification. You just can't wait to get that new iPhone, purse, or shoes. You feel like whenever you have money, you need to spend it. To reverse this, recognize you do this. The first step is honesty. Then formulate something that will help you delay the gratification and not mind waiting. For example, if I like to reward myself, I'll create a system where if I save $10,000, I reward myself for saving it. In the process, maybe I'm putting $500 away each month. I don't have $500 to spend, but I might have $50 to go get that bag which is a smaller reward each month. It's not that you can't ever get that luxury item. You just may need to wait until you get your properties first. It's about priorities.

Sometimes people are so used to their spending usage that they don't realize that they can simply reallocate their money to save the down payment for their first property. As an example, we had clients who had a 500 credit score and no money saved for their down payment. When we gave them a goal of saving $10,000, the wife thought we were crazy because they were living in their parent's basement with their two children sleeping in the closet. She was also expecting their third child.

With a little more digging into how they were budgeting their money, we noticed that their paycheck never lasted until the next payday, partially because over ten percent was being given to tithe. They had great hearts to be faithful servants here on Earth, but with our financial literacy guidance, they also came to understand that they needed to set an example for their children, God's greatest gift to them. They never realized that they could build their treasure in heaven and also give their children an abundant life too. All this time, they thought they had to choose.

Even though we lowered their tithe to ten percent, they were still giving generously to their church. We also had them set aside ten percent for savings. To ensure their success, we created an automatic transfer from their paycheck into a savings account that they wouldn't touch. The rest was available for other living expenses and spending. In just 16 weeks, they were able to purchase their first property and move out of mom and dad's basement!

If you're not disciplined enough to do it yourself, automating your savings process makes it easier to lay aside that money. Some people may have the option to ask their employer for two paychecks – one for twenty percent that goes directly into a savings account and the remainder into a regular checking account. Either way, it's important to lock in your savings every month.

The last savings topic that we want to touch on is saving for your kids' education. We met a man, whom, for privacy reasons, we will name Mr Fischer. Mr Fischer refused to save for his kids' college. It became a choice between their education or saving for his retirement. Mr Fischers' philosophy was to empower his kids by making them be responsible for their own student loans. He expressed that they were going to get married, start their own families, then wonder why they had to take care of him because he failed to plan for his retirement. Mr Fischer didn't want to put pressure on his kids to explain to their spouse, who may be from a different culture, the responsibility of having to sacrifice financially to support their dad. The kids may not feel obligated to send him $1000 a month just because he chose to sacrifice to fund their college. They may end up putting him in a home where he would rely on government assistance and funding and not have any money. Mr Fischer concluded that paying for his kids' college could be enabling a bad habit, so instead of saving for their university and college, he decided to plan for his retirement. He felt this course of action would encourage them not to get into unnecessary student debt as this would be their responsibility. When financed by the Bank of Mom and Dad, they don't have any skin in the game. Many times, as an immigrant, you just don't have that extra money. If you sacrifice to put your kids through school, will they understand that sacrifice enough to tell their spouse about their reciprocal obligation? Mr Fischer didn't want to leave this to chance.

RENT for cashflow

Most people don't think about their house as something that will pay them but you're going to know better. It's smart to invest in assets that pay you. Many immigrants will come to this country and get a job, buy the biggest house they can afford, along with a nice car just to show that they've made it. They're proud of what they've accomplished. What they miss is that those things are liabilities.

Let's get into the mindset of getting assets that pay you. Buying a house that can pay you may seem unusual but it's the way to build wealth. After you have a couple of those properties, you can move up to your own big dream house with the cash flow coming from your other homes. That's security. At the end of the day, if you buy that big house and the nice car with the income from your job and you lose your job, what happens? You are financing a lifestyle that is unsustainable and you may not be able to afford it. If you have properties paying you, you wouldn't need to worry about that at all.

If you are going to buy a house for yourself, our top tip is to make sure that you have an income-producing suite. That's called a "mortgage helper" which we will talk more about in a future chapter. It's no longer a full-on liability. You are supplementing your mortgage by having the tenant downstairs pay part of it. Oftentimes it's too soon to buy your first home without an income suite because you're open to risk if you lose your job.

The thing to remember is that properties become more valuable over time so you get to benefit from that in the future. You get tenants who are paying the rent which in turn pays your mortgage. That's a mortgage pay down. Now imagine 25 years from now when your tenant has fully paid for your house. Your house is worth more by then as well. At that point, if you decide you want to retire back home, you have a lot of choices.

1. Refinance, taking the cash out

2. Continue to have tenants paying you rent and live off the passive income
3. Sell the property

No matter which option, if you want to retire back home, you can probably buy yourself a nice house and have a good retirement there.

INCOME from employment

In general, we tend to talk about Return on Investment but we forget that there's also Return on Time, which is more important. If you get a Return on Investment that equals Return on Time, it's much better. This is really what we're working towards with real estate – to provide you with options for a better future. When you have assets producing cash flow, that money can be used to support your family instead of a job and buy back your time. You have more time with your kids, you have more time with your families, you have more time to travel, and to do the things you've always dreamed of doing.

Now don't get us wrong, getting a job is not bad. One of the biggest weapons you can have in acquiring assets is having a steady stream of income and a stable job because you will need to prove you are employed. If you are self employed, you will need to show a minimum of two years with steady income to buy your first property as well. The banks look more favourably upon having a 9-5 than being self employed or being an investor. It definitely helps you qualify for a mortgage.

We know this is a very different mentality than school teaches you. We've been raised to think we just need to be a good employee and trade our time for an hourly wage or a yearly salary and work our way up the corporate ladder. We need to flip the switch on this.

So, here's the plan: you get a job so you can save money and get your first mortgage. Then you take your income and invest it in assets. After a period of time, the cash flow from those assets will replace your working income and then you have the option to quit your job or chase your other passions. When you think of a job like this, it's temporary. It's a means to an end. Your sacrifice of working two to three jobs is only for a few years instead of until retirement.

CREDIT management

Colleen

I was really excited when I got my first credit card. It had a $5000 credit limit and originally, this was an emergency fund for me but it so happened there was a family emergency. My family had a need for exactly the same amount that was on my credit card and I felt guilty not helping out. If you're an immigrant, you understand that we always feel obligated to the family we left back home. The general perception is that living abroad makes you automatically rich. I couldn't pay the card because I was completing my education for the next three years, so that card eventually went to collections.

I could say that the lesson I learned was to only give what I can afford, which at times means to say no to family, but it was more than that. I honestly felt like I was sitting on $5000, but that $5000 wasn't really mine to give away. That is not what your credit limit means. I had no way to pay it back. In the end, no matter who takes the money from your card, it's your responsibility to pay it back, especially because it might be at 21.99% or more interest.

Zeb

My story with credit cards was that I made a mess out of them. I got the first credit card and I had no idea what it was really for, so I used it. I ended up getting three more. Then I found out when we tried to buy a house that I had to pay all of them back. Luckily, we never went into bankruptcy. We worked multiple jobs to pay those creditors and negotiated with collections so we could pay off every single card and repair our credit. Because everything was so far back, it didn't take too long after clearing our credit to get our first property. Initially, we tried to buy in March of 2011 and were denied, but after dedicating ourselves to paying things off, we were able to purchase our first property in November of 2012.

Whenever people come to us wanting our help, the first thing we usually talk about is getting their finances in order. If you're going to get a credit card, don't get excited and go on a shopping spree. Don't forget this is really a loan and it needs to be paid back. On the statements, you should really keep your eye on when your payments are due and what your minimums are. Worst case you want to really make sure that you're maintaining those minimums. Ideally, you want to pay more to tackle the debt.

Sometimes people can get completely scared of credit cards, especially after hearing some horror stories from others, but forget that you need credit to qualify for a mortgage. Certain loan types need two or three credit lines for approval. While there are credit lines other than credit cards, if you manage your credit cards well, it can help boost your credit score and more lenders will want to lend to you.

When using credit cards, you will want to stay under 30% usage or have a few credit cards that you don't use. The amount of credit you use as compared to your available credit is called your credit utilization rate. If you're looking at building your credit, go ahead and buy your bag of chips, swipe your credit card, then move over to the side and pay your credit card right away. Apps and online banking make this really easy these days. Those multiple payments every month can help build your credit history because it shows you have an ongoing multiple payment pattern every month.

For example, let's say you buy ten bags of chips throughout the month because you just love chips that much. Instead of making one lump sum payment at the end of the month, make ten smaller payments immediately after. This will help build your credit better than the one-time monthly payment.

There are three major credit reporting agencies: Experian, Equifax, and Transunion. They report consumer spending and paying habits. While sometimes the information reported by each may be different, there are five main areas they look at to calculate a credit score:

1. Payment history
2. Total amount owed
3. Length of credit history
4. Types of credit
5. New credit

Make sure you have a credit card bill in your name that you're consistently paying on time. No matter what kind of bill you have, make sure you're consistently paying it on time. When the creditors look at your profile, they will evaluate how consistent you are in paying your bills, so that they can trust you with higher ticket items. If you show the banks that you can deal well with smaller things, then they know they can trust you with bigger things too.

In case you've had a bankruptcy in the past, it can create some limits in your life. For example, in Canada, it would take seven years for it to fall off your credit report.

We will share more about the story of when we tried to buy our first property in a later chapter. The short story is we got denied. Our credit wasn't high enough for the mortgage requirements and that's when it hit us that a decision we made five years ago was still haunting us. We had the down payment. We felt like we had everything ready to go, but we weren't able to buy a house because of a lapse of judgment years ago with our credit. This is why it's so important to share this in the financial literacy section so you're not surprised like we were when you go to buy your first property.

KNOWLEDGE growth

It all begins and ends with education. Whether you got up to grade 12 or graduated from university, get enough education so that you can be well versed in any industry you may want to get into.

From there, it's all about investing in more of your education. We live in a system where we think the only type of education we can get is from schools, but if you want to be financially free, you might realize that school education may not be enough or right for you. Remember there are many examples of millionaires like Mark Zuckerberg or Elon Musk who dropped out of school. We've been too slow in embracing other ways of getting an education or thinking that working a regular nine to five job until you retire will get you all you need and want.

When we talk about education in this book, we are talking about getting educated in what you want in life, also known as specialized education. Follow someone who's doing what you want to do. Regardless, if you choose to follow us or someone else who has achieved what you want to achieve, get educated or learn from them. When you do that, it cuts your learning curve; it's exactly what we did when we got our mentor five years ago. Imagine if you would have succeeded on your own in five years, you can now fast track what you want in just two years instead because you're following a proven blueprint.

Chapter 3

Becoming Your Own Bank

Zeb

If you remember, we shared earlier we paid $20,000 to learn about real estate from our mentor. We knew we would get that investment back many times over and we did, but the only way we could do this was with a credit card. Once we were ready knowledge-wise to start investing, we realized we did not have the money for down payments. But what we learned from the initial $20,000 investment is that it gave us an idea to leverage our credit cards so we could buy as many properties as we wanted. This is the idea of using other people's money. We used the bank's money to put down payments on these properties. Then with the cash flow we made from these properties, we paid back the credit cards, which were later converted to Lines of Credit for lower interest payment, keeping the difference as profit.

This is why knowing and calculating the interest rates is really important. You need to look at the interest rate you're paying on the card and calculate how much cash flow you need to make in order for the whole transaction to make sense. The great thing is if you can get the zero percent offers on your credit cards, you're not paying anything but the transaction fee to have that money right now. Whether you pay it back in six, eight or twelve months, you have the ability to use the money to make more money. After your zero interest time is up, you have made it all back plus some. So for us, our journey in real estate was helped a lot by credit cards and we've continued to grow by using them.

Please know we are not saying to be reckless with credit cards. We've already talked about being smart with them in previous chapters and the mistakes we made. Do not take this strategy as permission to create bad habits or overspend. If you're someone who has struggled with credit cards and has not yet figured out how to use them to your advantage, this may not be your best tactic to get properties.

The interest on some cards can be very high, over twenty percent, but sometimes you can call the bank that issued the card and negotiate down the rate. Thing is, you have to be willing to make the call. The rate you can get depends on a few factors. It may be according to different cards the bank has and their policy on switching back and forth or on your credit score, so if your credit score has increased, that's even more reason to give the bank a call. The higher your credit score, the more options and negotiating power you have with the banks.

Most people just go online and look at the credit cards that are available but that's not the only way to find a card. You can also call the banks to find out what kinds of offers they have and when you hear their offers, take into consideration the benefits that come with the cards. Some of them will give you reward points, travel perks, cash back, bonuses, etc. in addition to low or zero percent rates. Another way to use Other People's Money (OPM) is by getting a line of credit from your bank or, if you own a home already, you can refinance and get cash out through an equity line of credit. Still some of our investors have been known to take money out of their retirement accounts to invest and pay themselves back instead.

You may be wondering how to know if the deal you're getting is a good deal. This is where the concept of cash on cash return comes in. How much money are you getting back by using other people's money? What is the minimum target goal that makes sense for your situation? To calculate your cash on cash return for a five percent down property of $100,000, take the cash flow per month, after all expenses, multiply by 12 months and divide it by your initial $5000 down payment. This is then the percent you're earning each year from that $5000 investment. We will go into a full example calculation in Part 3, but for now, the formula is this:

Cash on Cash Return:

$$\frac{\text{Annual Cashflow}}{\text{Down Payment/Initial Investment}} = \text{Percent return on investment per year}$$

In contrast, by using the rule of 72 which says the number of years it will take your money to double is equal to 72 divided by your percentage rate, investing $5000 in the bank at two percent per year would take 36 years to double.

Rule of 72:

$$\frac{72}{2} = \text{Number of years for investment to double}$$

Let's say you buy a property for zero down and hold it for five years. What kind of return could you make on this investment? Here's a simple example:

Price: $100,000
Appreciation: $2,100 per year at two percent appreciation
Years you keep the house: 5
Total Appreciation after 5 years: $10,500
Amount of mortgage paid down from the tenant (a.k.a Mortgage Paydown): $16,014.00
Gross profit: $10,500 + $16,014.00 = $26,514.00

Purchase Price:	$100,000.00	Holding Term:	5 years
Passive Appreciation:	$16,014.00	Calculated at two percent per year X holding time (5years)	
Mortgage Paydown:	$10,500.00	We use a mortgage calculator to find exact principal payment	http://bit.ly/ mcalculate
Cashflow:	$0.00	May not be any if this is acquired at $0 down and you live in one of the units	
Active Appreciation:	$0.00	We will assume no renos were added to increase value	
Gross Profit:	**$26,514.00**		

After yearly expenses and realtor fees, you could walk away with about $15,000.00 after five years on a property for which you put nothing down. This does not include any rental income obtained while renting any part of the house.

Colleen

Another way we're becoming our own bank is through life insurance. We're purchasing universal life insurance for our kids. From the time they were two weeks old, we've been putting $100 a month towards their policy. That also assures us they'll never be disqualified for insurance and when they're older, they can borrow from the insurance policy and use it as a down payment to purchase a home, or they could use it as their student loan. We do this because we realize it's true there are two things guaranteed in life – death and taxes.

Life insurance is something many people, especially immigrants, don't think about very much. It's something we have seen over and over again where someone passes away and they leave nothing and have no insurance. This, in turn, will lead their loved ones needing to source funeral funds through the gofundme platform They could be asking for donations of over $15,000 and this is one big reason why it's important to be insured.

While we are not licensed financial advisors and everyone's situation is different, in general, we like getting universal life insurance because it is also an investment vehicle. Because everyone's needs are different, please make sure to consult your financial advisor to get specific advice on your needs. Feel free to also contact us on our website at www.thetsikiras.com for who we work with.

While you may have heard of the more common term or whole life policies, universal life gives you a completely different set of benefits that appealed to us. Universal life insurance builds cash value and has flexible payment options. Unlike term life that ends, which would be the equivalent to renting, universal life insurance covers you for your entire life. It also earns interest on your account unlike regular whole life insurance.[1]

Being able to change the premium and the death benefit amount without getting a new policy (may need new underwriting or incur costs) can be a pro for some. Even though you have a premium, you can use the policy's own cash value to pay the premium. So if you have enough cash value, you can skip your payment all together. Policy holders can also access a portion of the cash value without affecting the guaranteed death benefit. One thing to note is that universal life insurance's interest rate is sensitive to current market interest rates. If the interest rate decreases to the minimum rate, your premium would need to increase to offset the reduced cash value.[2]

If you do end up withdrawing a cash portion, you will be taxed additionally. You can also borrow against the accumulated cash value without tax implications, but you will pay interest on the loan amount and a cash surrender fee. Unpaid loans will reduce the death benefit. And the thing you may not like is that upon the death of the insured, the insurance company will keep the remaining cash value that is above the death benefit being paid to the beneficiaries.

As you age, make sure you're keeping up with the rising cost of insurance because there could be a time where there is not enough cash value to keep the policy in force unless you pay higher premiums.[3]

Another reason we like universal life is you can use your policy after retirement. The cash value account accumulates tax free. "Some people use the cash value in their life insurance policy to bridge the gap from [the year of their] retirement to age 70 when they can receive the highest Social Security benefit," says David Wilken, former president of Individual Life Sales for Voya Financial.

"In general, the more time you allow your cash-value life insurance policy to grow, the better," adds Wilken. "A good rule of thumb is to plan to wait at least 15 years [after you purchase a policy] before you begin taking distributions."[4]

Chapter 4

The Accidental House Hacker

Colleen

We happened upon "House Hacking" by accident when we moved to northern Canada. Zeb was staying in a three bedroom apartment with two others paying $800 per month for his room. Because I was moving to be with him, that wasn't going to work anymore. We met a man who was moving out of his two bedroom apartment who said he would let us take over his lease. We thought this was a great help to us as we didn't need to go through the normal apartment rental application process. But there was one condition -- he had already rented out the other bedroom. We would be living with a complete stranger.

I was a little hesitant at first, but we decided to give it a shot because it was just going to be around six months. A few months later, my brother and Zeb's friend wanted to move to our city. However when you talk about traveling to a new place, the first thing that comes to mind is accommodations and the two needed our help in that regard.

We offered them our living room and we knew we had to sell it to our roommate. The reason it made sense was because we understood we would all save extra money. So we asked our roommate what he thought about cutting his rent. Our guests would pay a third of the monthly rent and that would lower our roommate's contribution too. This is how we discovered house hacking.

At the end of our 6 month term, our roommate decided to take over the lease. We had to look for a new apartment. We were determined not to get another roommate. As the only woman living with four other men, the previous situation was not ideal. We all worked the same shift so you can imagine what it was like. We were newlyweds and wanted our privacy.

Our First Tenant

We realized how limited our choices were when we started looking for a new apartment. Since our community population was just 20,000 people and mostly transient, there was near zero vacancy. So we decided to contact a big REIT in town to see what they had. They told us there was only one apartment available.

As we drove up, the apartment complex looked in shambles. People had their clothes hanging outside. The apartment carried musty smells which suspiciously reeked of urine. We figured that there must have been vagrants who frequented the common areas of the building. It felt like we had hit a new rock bottom. We were sure we wouldn't like it there, so we started to negotiate our way out of seeing the apartment. The problem was there was nothing else and she told us if we didn't take this, she wouldn't have anything else available for months.

We were told the unit had been recently renovated and it actually turned out to be really nice inside. When we entered the unit I immediately saw the big windows. I could see the grass and the trees as our unit faced the hills and open space. Coming from a two bedroom shared apartment, this felt Zen. It had a nice linoleum floor. The bathroom was decent. There was a galley kitchen. We were glad that we were open to seeing it. Really, it was because there was no other option and the outside curb appeal surely would've sent us back in a different direction.

So again, we went for a two-bedroom concept with the idea that the second bedroom would be a guest bedroom. The lease was for a year, which was longer than we initially wanted, but we decided to ride the wave. We were happy to have our own space and really excited to have it all to ourselves. It was a great thought until a friend came to us and asked if we would rent our second room to his friend. Instinctively, we responded that our second bedroom was for guests, not to rent. But when he said his friend was desperate and would pay half of our rent, we realized we couldn't call ourselves much of investors if we turned this opportunity down. So we decided to give up our privacy one more time. Besides, it would only be for three months.

Zeb

At around that same time, we met an older couple who called us their kids. The Chumas had been living in the city for a few years and, like many others, were working three to four jobs. One day, Mrs Chuma logged into her bank account to inspire us as she showed us how proud they were that they had saved up $50,000. Mrs Chuma was *disappointed in our lack of drive as she exclaimed there was no reason why we would be mediocre and not working as hard as they were.*

Mrs Chuma shared how she and her husband had agreed to a plan where they would each earn $4000 every two weeks. In order to do that, they needed to work all those jobs. Colleen and I decided we could do the same thing. There was no reason a couple our parents' age could do that and we couldn't. If they could save 50 percent of their income, we could too. That inspired us and reignited the need of pushing and doing a lot more than we were doing as we realized we were getting comfortable by turning tenants away for privacy.

A couple of months later our tenant left as he had found an apartment elsewhere. At that point it was just automatic for us to list the room. We put out an ad describing this beautiful two bedroom newly renovated suite. Our first person of interest was someone coming from out of town. They were coming for work but because they weren't in town yet, they had a friend come to look at the property.

Our potential tenant's friend managed to brave herself to get into the building. She walked into the apartment and said, "Wow, this is nice. I did not expect it. I was wondering what Terry was thinking when she sent me this address to come look at this place. I can really see how you guys have made it very homey." We had decorated the place and furnished the second bedroom. We actually made the rented room look more comfortable than our own room because we understood this was an investment.

She immediately texted Terry that the place was tastefully decorated and we were a lovely couple who she was going to love, especially since Terry didn't have many friends in town. As she walked out the door, we heard our phones beep as we received an email transfer. That was the damage deposit needed to secure the room. And that is how we started our whole journey towards becoming investors and renting out rooms. Terry went on to rent from us for months and later moved into one of our investment properties.

Chapter 5

Let Go of Comfort and Fear

If you're an immigrant or if you're someone who has never been taught financial literacy, what we've shared so far may seem new or even overwhelming. It was overwhelming to us too. Remember, we had to learn about our checkbooks and credit after college. But we took it little by little, learning one thing, then learning the next thing and over time, we finally got to the point where we can now share that knowledge with you. Our students have been the same and come with different levels of financial literacy. Watching them grow and succeed in this area has been one of our biggest blessings in life.

We know that people tend to revert back to their comfort zones when something new is placed in front of them. It's somewhat human nature. It feels easier and less scary to deal with what you know than what you don't, but if you always stay in your comfort zone, you'll never grow. It's okay to feel whatever you feel but give yourself a deadline to be done with it. Whether it's a five minute limit or a little longer, the way to combat any hesitation is to just get into action.

Having fear is normal and we would be more surprised if you told us you had no fears about starting your journey to financial freedom and generational wealth. It's what you do with that fear that makes all the difference. Will you let it run you, paralyze you, and keep you playing small? Or will you use it as fuel to take your next steps?

"Fear and excitement are actually the same feeling. And it's a feeling you can control. Every single time you feel afraid, you can feel EXCITED instead." ~ Mel Robbins

Think back to the first time you drove a car. How scared were you? What about going in reverse or parallel parking? But the more you drove, the better you became. Turning left may have meant waiting for a huge gap in traffic back then, whereas now, you easily turn without hesitation. Maybe you parked way out in the parking lot so you didn't have to be next to other cars. Now you squeeze into small spots without a problem. That's exactly how it has been for us in the last few years. So don't worry, it's normal to have whatever feelings you have. Just don't let it hold you back because we know you can be successful too.

If success was easy, everybody would be achieving it. You need to get out of your comfort zone. If your top goal is to be comfortable, then you're going to stay where you are right now. We don't know any examples of people that used staying safe as a way to succeed in life. Dreams come true from getting out of your comfort zone.

In assisting you to overcome your fear, we would want to understand what's driving it. As an example, we were dealing with a student who was anxious about renting out her basement suite. Lisa has a basement apartment in her home. Just the thought of having someone else in her space triggered her anxiety. So we asked what she was scared of -- what's the worst that could happen? Then we tackled each issue. She said she was scared the tenant would come upstairs. The question is how to make her feel more comfortable. If one lock on the outside doesn't do it, she can install three. She can add an alarm system that separates the upstairs from the downstairs so that even if that tenant somehow got so crafty they went upstairs, the alarm would notify her there's someone coming up.

So when we coach our students, we go through their fears one by one to understand them. If you're worried somebody is going to trash your property, would it be helpful for you to pay a little more for insurance? Then if a tenant was to trash the place it would be covered. If you're scared the place will get burned down, then get tenant insurance that covers it and make sure your tenants have insurance, which covers their belongings. Most fears come from a lack of knowledge. When you uncover them and find a solution, the fear goes away.

Tony Robbins talks about walking on fire or jumping into a pool of freezing water every morning to tackle your fears. Everything starts from fear, but fear has two meanings: Forget Everything And Run or Face Everything And Rise. All you need to do is figure out which part of fear is holding you back so you can overcome it and create a clearer path to the lifestyle you desire.

Part 2:
Your Mortgage
Helper

Chapter 6

From No Rent to $2.75M Deal

We just wrote an offer on a $2.75M property and put down a $20,000 earnest money deposit. Even though it sounds cliché, getting here started with a dream. We made goals, we dug our heads in the sand and we charted the course to achieve them. As time went on, we gained momentum and now, sitting down to write an offer on a 21 unit apartment building feels incredible and absolutely amazing.

A short ten years ago, we didn't even have rent money. Some people ask us how we did it and we often talk about focus. If you focus on what you want, you'll get there. Admittedly, we lost focus early on but then realized that we had to get back on track if we wanted the dream. Just know the voice that fuels your dreams must be louder than any other voice you hear.

There were definitely people who told us we were crazy. They pleaded with us to just do something "normal." People wondered why we needed to dream like this. Then we were told we couldn't do it – that we were just a couple of immigrants trying to make it big. Who did we think we were? It was too expensive to get into real estate and there was no way we could achieve it. Our family even told us that no one in the family had ever been in real estate so why did we think we were so special?

Once we got more successful, the criticism changed. We were told we were working too much. We weren't spending enough time with each other and our kids. We even heard, "You're going to get divorced if you don't slow down!"

Zeb

When I dropped out of school, I remember telling myself I failed and that I was going to end up being exactly what I was running away from, my father. My dad wasn't a bad person. After selling everything my parents had and coming to Canada as immigrants, I saw how hard he worked. I witnessed the nights he was in too much pain to get back to his dishwashing job and how he hopped from one agency to another. I would say to myself that my parents sacrificed everything so we can have a chance at a good future and I needed to make them proud.

There usually is one needy person in each family who can't quite seem to get their life together. I thought I would end up being that person, but also knew that I would always wonder if I didn't take this chance. It definitely felt scary, it was nothing like I've ever done before, but at that time of my life, I cared more about the dream than I did about being scared.

It feels so commonplace when we buy a new property nowadays. We know the process inside and out. We know what to look for, which questions to ask, and what to expect. Now, I can't even describe how it feels to live the life which I used to dream of back then. In a way, I didn't even really know what I was dreaming about then to even attempt to imagine the feeling. I couldn't envision sitting down to sign an offer for $2.75M ten years ago. All I knew was that I wanted to be successful in real estate investing.

Back when we were starting with multiple properties, our accounting got out of hand. We were trying to do it all on our own. We had to log the expenses and keep track of everything. Unfortunately, we didn't have a great system which made it feel more stressful and overwhelming than it needed to be. We started to wonder, is this really worth it? Do we want to continue at this pace? We had to get an accountant to help us which alleviated a lot of the burden.

Once our accounting and systems were in place, we got to the point that we were ready to expand. We had fourteen doors and wanted to grow even more. One cold -50°C morning, we were planning our yearly winter getaway to a sunny destination. Our criteria included: within a 5hr flight, family friendly, tourist destination and ability to purchase at an affordable price to then list as a short term rental. Our goal was to combine our love for travel and real estate. This eliminated all of Canada so we decided to start investing internationally. Our search landed us in Phoenix and Scottsdale, Arizona. We weren't familiar with the areas, we didn't know a real estate agent, and we had no connections to any mortgage brokers. We were just free spirits allowing our love for travel to guide and influence our next purchase. Without much of a plan, two weeks later, we were in Phoenix in February on a 3 week vacation. What we hadn't realized was that our travel dates fell right in the midst of peak season. With only the first 4 nights booked and our host letting us know we couldn't extend due to full occupancy, we packed our bags and 2 kids as we hopped from Airbnb to Airbnb. Within 3 weeks, we had viewed over 70 properties, made 5 offers then closed on 2! This was the start of our Real Estate Investing Roadtrip. For every new city we visited and invested in, it felt like starting over again. We were taking a chance on the research we had done on the city including the market cycle, economic drivers, housing supply & demand and consumer confidence. We based our buying decisions on facts, not our emotions, but it still felt a little scary.

Chapter 7

Your First Home Should be an Investment Property

There's a difference in buying your first personal home and buying your first home as an investment property. In the first scenario, it's the place in which you're living. In the second scenario, you have a different purpose when buying that first home – you want to look at it as an investment with an income suite.

What if your property could pay you? Most people don't think of their first home in this way, but when you buy a property that doesn't pay you, you are buying a liability. Yes, that house that you bought as a place to live in is a liability. You are using your working income to pay that mortgage. However, if you can buy a property that has two suites, you can put a tenant in one suite and you can live in the other. You can also rent out rooms too, if you don't have separate suites.

Don't worry if you don't find many properties set up for this. Even if you already own your home, you can convert it. If you're up for the project, you can even do it yourself -- it will increase the value of your home and you will now own a property with an income suite. Just make sure to research any property you look at to ensure it has the potential to be the income-generating house you think it could be. Don't forget to also look at your city's bylaws to make sure you're in compliance with the rules and regulations.

If you have the second suite, you have what we call your "mortgage helper". That income suite will help you offset your living costs and put more money in your pocket. That means you'll be able to get into your next investment property quicker than if you paid the entire mortgage on your own.

There are even some investors who use the strategy of buying a property at 5% down and moving every few years. Every couple of years they'll buy a fourplex and live in one unit while renting out the other three. Just so you know, anything up to four units is considered a residential property and won't need special commercial loans. This is why the fourplex is so attractive to some investors because the more units you have, the more income you can generate.

You may be wondering how to know whether owning multi-units is for you? We have had students and clients in very different situations and you will need to analyze it for yourself. If you ask a family of five to buy a fourplex and move into one unit, it may not be big enough. They may not want to make the sacrifice. How many families with three kids or even just two would move into a three bed one bath unit? In other cases, some people can't afford to buy a single family home in the city they really want to live in. In these scenarios, the best solution would be to buy a fourplex and rent out all four units provided you have a sufficient downpayment. Your family would then rent and live in a house somewhere else, but that fourplex is paying the rent on the house. With this concept, the idea is to buy where you can rent out and rent where you want to live.

One thing to note is that if you do have a primary residence in your fourplex, your capital gains tax will be lower at time of sale. Your fourplex will be considered your primary residence. If you don't live there, it will be considered a rental property and taxed at a higher rate. This is exactly why some investors prefer to move into the house when the exit strategy is to sell.

For most people, getting a fourplex right away as a first time home buyer and investor is not the most affordable. You have to be earning a good salary and be able to prove that you have a steady income. Most of the time people will start with a duplex or a single family home they can convert, then work their way up to the fourplex. If you can afford it right away, we think the fourplex is a great way to create higher cash flow.

Realistically, you never know until you ask your mortgage broker if it would work for you. They just might surprise you and say yes to your loan. So don't make assumptions. Ask first. With some creativity and flexibility, you might be able to afford the fourplex sooner than you think.

Don't Make Assumptions about Your Property

Doing your research is very important in whatever area you want to buy. Make sure you check the zoning of the property itself. What are you allowed to do and what are you not allowed to do? Ask the realtor, do your own research, or check with the city. For example, some cities have banned short term rentals like Airbnb. If you're going to be buying your property and thinking of doing short term rentals, it's very important that you know if the city allows it. And if they allow it, what rules do you have to follow? Do you need a business license, fire inspection or any other permits? What is or isn't allowed? And then from there, you can make an informed decision.

You'll also want to research how much rent you can get for a property. Every city has different average rents and you don't want to put so much into upgrades or construction that you can't make a profit. Different cities also have varying prices for contract labour. We could put a blanket number on it like $50,000 but every city and every situation is different. Just run the numbers to make sure the investment makes sense. For example, in Vancouver, $150,000 won't get you much. In Toronto, $50,000 won't get you much either. But $50,000 in Detroit or Cleveland could renovate or buy an entire house.

The best advice we can give you during the due diligence stage is:
1. Obtain a property inspection
2. Research city bylaws
3. Obtain a quote for renovations were applicable -- get three quotes from local contractors
4. Contact a property manager and find out their thoughts on rents
5. Place a phantom ad to test the market

When complete, you will know if the property has good potential for you to invest in. You also want to check when you're applying for a mortgage if your mortgage company or lender can lend you the improvement (renovation) money that you need. Then you don't have to try to get another loan or pay out of pocket for improvements.

If you can't get your mortgage lender to approve the improvements, you'll need to decide whether you're going to use a line of credit or other methods. For example, think about where and how you would get $50,000. If it's from a credit card at 19.99% interest and your Return On Investment (ROI) is only eight percent, it doesn't make any sense. Again, always run the numbers. Every scenario is unique and making changes to a single family house may not make as much sense as getting a duplex or suited home (house with a basement suite).

When people run the numbers on multiple properties and are not getting instant results, they can sometimes start to think this type of investing doesn't work or they give up. But it's like any type of business. You have to keep looking and keep running the numbers until you find something that serves your purpose and makes sense. Don't be impatient to get something. Don't run on emotions and fall in love with a house and be impulsive. When you hit that gem, it will be worth the wait. This patience and perseverance is what makes a successful investor.

Here in Canada, you generally need to put down five percent on your principal residence. For example, if you have a property for $350,000, you'll be required to put down $17,500. There are people who find it difficult to save that amount of money, so all of a sudden, they feel like they are just cut off from the investment property ladder. This is when you need to get creative. How can you get in without that much money? Don't lose hope – there are other ways to get properties. If there's a will, there's a way.

Creative Financing

When people don't have the money to invest in real estate right away, they need to find other ways to aggressively save or they need to get creative in the ways that they approach home sellers. We've found that the latter is very useful and homeowners are more open to it than you might think. You can offer homeowners a deal in such a way that you don't have to get a mortgage today. You don't have to transfer the property into your name today. Instead, you put together an Agreement for Sale so that you can transfer it in three to five years.

In this scenario, you take over the seller's mortgage payments. Both parties agree on a purchase price today and an initial deposit. You also take care of the taxes and maintenance. You take care of the house like it's your own house. The only difference is the house is not in your name today. It will be in three to five years. The advantage of doing an Agreement for Sale is that you're paying the mortgage directly to the owner. You get the benefit of the mortgage pay down. Then in three to five years when the agreement matures, you will buy that property at the balance of the mortgage. When you do an Agreement for Sale, you have the ability to transact with the house as if it's your own including having a power of attorney to sell it.

Some people prefer to offer Rent To Own (RTO) agreements to the homeowner. Some rent to own deals may still ask for a down payment, but it's negotiable. Then you can be as creative as you want. Maybe you don't have the whole five percent down so you ask if you can spread out the down payment over five to eight years. Maybe you start with $5000 to get into this agreement and then every year you give the seller another $5000 until you reach that down payment amount. This is in addition to your monthly payment. Then in five years when you buy this property, you would have accumulated extra money paid in. When you do these types of rent to own deals, you get a lease and then you also get the Rent to Own Agreement.

The only difference between the Agreement For Sale on its own and a Rent to Own deal is that you buy the property at today's price. With the Rent to Own, you buy the property based on what we think the property is going to be worth in year five. It's just a matter of asking enough people who are selling to find somebody who says yes because some homeowners aren't even aware they can do this. And those that do know don't advertise that they're open to this type of financing deal.

Many of us say no to a new idea instinctively, so when you present these types of creative financing deals, expect to hear no first. Understand that what they really mean is that they need to feel more comfortable with the process. In fact, in sales, it's common for a customer to say no five times before saying yes. This is because people buy with their emotions first, then justify their decision with logic.

When people evaluate decisions, they usually go through all the reasons not to say yes first. Just like when you get tested for medical conditions, the doctor is trying to rule out things (say no) rather than confirm an ailment. Many decisions are either pain avoidance or pleasure-seeking so a no, for someone who should be saying yes, is usually based on:

1. Incomplete information: they need more details to get clarity or they need an explanation in a way they can understand
2. More time: some people like to "sleep on" things and others need time to run through scenarios in their head.
3. Either say: these people say no in order to buy themselves more time.
4. Unfavorable circumstances: something out of their control is standing in their way. You may or may not be able to help them get past this issue.

Analyze 100 Properties

The rule of thumb we share with our students is that you want to analyze 100 properties. Make sure that the numbers work for what you're looking for. Go visit ten, make three offers and expect one to be accepted. If you think it sounds like a lot, just think of Walt Disney going to approximately 300 banks in order for us to have Disney World like it is today. Or if you think about Kentucky Fried Chicken (KFC), Colonel Harland Sanders was turned down 1009 times with his recipe before his KFC chicken was accepted.

Every coin has two sides: you could look at it as an opportunity or you could look at it as a challenge. If investing in real estate is truly what you want, you have a fire inside you to become financially free, and investing creatively is your only option as you don't qualify traditionally, you will analyze 100 properties, go see ten, offer on three and find the one. If it doesn't work just keep going. Do the numbers. Just like anything in sales, you just need to keep going. Inevitably, if you keep at it, you will find one that works for you. Don't stop digging -- you're usually only three feet from gold.

When you're narrowing down which 100 properties to be creative with, look at the properties that have been on the MLS listings for hundreds of days. Go from the oldest to the newest. If the listing has sat there for a while, they're likely more willing to listen to something more creative. There are even realtors who know about these creative offers. But you have to have a seller who is open and wanting to get rid of their property. You may have to educate them and sometimes those end up being the best deals.

The good news for realtors is that even with an Agreement for Sale, they still get paid. So it's not as if you're cutting out the realtor. The realtor will still make the commission, sometimes double. A sale is still considered a sale. For example, let's say we do an Agreement for Sale on a property. When it's sold, the seller pays the commission. Then, years down the line, if we don't close with the seller, the seller will have to list again and that will be another sale for the realtor. A knowledgeable realtor can facilitate that and that's why it's important to know who you're working with and pick a great investor focused realtor.

The realtor interviews (list of our recommended questions are in Part 3) are very important because you want to know that your realtor can get creative in getting that mortgage. Don't forget that in these situations, it's important to have a lawyer who understands and can help with these types of deals too. You don't want to get to the point that the seller has agreed and you don't have a lawyer who can draw up the paperwork. So you want to make sure that all this is lined up because when you are talking to a seller who doesn't know about creative financing, they'll have a lot of questions that you'll want to be able to answer. Having the right realtor and lawyer on your team is critical.

There was a time when we found a property that fit all the criteria of what we were looking for. Our realtor approached the seller and asked if they would be open to an Agreement for Sale. The seller said, "Not a chance." This property ticked all the boxes and had been on the market a long time. The seller was no longer living in the property. It fit all the reasons why an Agreement for Sale would be perfect. Our realtor knew that the seller was saying no, not because he wasn't interested, but because he was misinformed or uninformed. The seller didn't know what the advantages of the Agreement for Sale were.

Our realtor gave him a brochure with information on what an Agreement for Sale is and recommended that the seller speak to a lawyer. It wasn't helping that his realtor also had no idea what an Agreement for Sale was. The seller came back saying that his lawyer also told him "No" and said "There is way too much risk associated with doing an Agreement for Sale. You're going to have problems. Don't do it."

Our realtor asked if he could introduce him to another lawyer who specializes in Agreement for Sale deals. Maybe his understanding and the way he'll explain it to you will help. They agreed and, after the conversation with that lawyer, they agreed to meet us. We sat down and negotiated terms and we were able to show them that we were responsible people who wanted to purchase this property. We went over the payment plan and how we planned to take care of the property at the agreed upon terms. After that conversation they were ready to go.

This example shows how people can be distrustful or worried about something that they just don't have all the information on or haven't heard of before. Sometimes they say no because they don't know better. Give them a chance to learn. Don't take it as a shut door. At times you just have to inform them or educate them on what it is they don't know by sending them to a qualified professional who will explain the concept to them in the right way. They might not listen to you, as a biased party explaining it to them, but they'll likely listen to a lawyer. Then they can see how it makes sense for them to do the deal. So choose your team wisely.

The great things about doing an Agreement for Sale is that you and the seller get to decide on the down payment. When you go to the bank, they dictate that amount and there is no negotiation. You have no choice. If the bank sets the downpayment at $20,000, they need the $20,000, whereas when you're dealing with people and being creative, you can make your own offer at a down payment amount that works for you.

Inspections

We want to emphasize again just how important getting an inspection can be. If you don't get an inspection done, you could end up in a situation where you've purchased a property only to find out it has a foundation problem. That's a big ticket item. Home purchasing is one of the largest purchases that a person can make in their lifetime – you want to make sure you are protected. Do not try to save a little money by skipping the inspection. There are so many things that we may not see or have the expertise to notice. Spend the $500 or $600 to get an inspection to make sure that your investment is secure.

We even recommend inspections on brand new properties. Some realtors will tell you that you don't need an inspection because a property is a condo or townhouse. Taking that advice is a big mistake. We recommend hundred percent of the time to have an inspection.

In fact, we have a friend who bought a new construction home and didn't do a home inspection in hopes of having no issues. Winter came along and she wondered why it was so cold in the house. She got married two years later and decided to sell the house. It was only then that she discovered the builder had never put insulation in the attic. Talk about literally throwing money out the chimney heating the house. She had no idea to check. She didn't have an inspection done since it was a new build. Luckily, the builder came back and put the insulation in for the new homebuyer without any issues.

Preplanning your Retirement

When you purchase properties, also create a plan for your
retirement. Let's say you want to retire in 20 years. There
are many exit strategies.

1. You can liquidate the property at that time.
2. You can sell the property, move back home (your
   country), buy a house there then live off the
   balance of your investment.
3. You can keep a property, hire a property manager,
   refinance then live off your investment.
4. You can leave a property for your kids and future
   generations.

No matter which option you choose, just be sure to
consider your exit strategy.

The non-immediate-liquidity of properties can be a pro for
some real estate investors who tend to be more impulsive
with their money. You can't spend it if you can't get to it,
right? When you put your money into real estate, you can't
wake up one day and say you want to buy a fancy new car
or luxury purse. That money is locked in an asset. If you
decide you want to refinance your property to get cash out,
it will take time and you'll have time to re-think your
purchase and determine if it's a need or a want.

Not having immediate access to your money can be a
good thing because five years from today, you will still
have those assets. By then you would have access to 20%
or more in equity. If you follow the recommendation we
gave to one client on making extra mortgage payments
into their property, it may be half paid off. We usually talk
about not locking money within your four walls because

you want to make sure that you can buy more assets. However, it's very important to know yourself and if you're someone whose money burns a hole in your pocket, let's redirect that money onto your mortgage and expedite paying off your home so that it is 100 percent free and clear.

So often immigrants will get that phone call where someone back home says there's an emergency. You need to know that their emergency is not yours to fix. It's great to have close family ties, but you shouldn't enable them to overly rely on you. It's okay to say no when a relative says they need $20,000 because they need a truck to start a new business. Plus, if your money is tied up in property assets, the process of refinancing your property gives you an opportunity to think. Is this how I want to spend my money? Is this actually a good idea? This is another reason why having non-liquid assets helps. If you have the liquid funds, it's easy to go to Western Union and send it. With the systems in place now, you can send this directly from your bank account in the comfort of your home. Maybe it's not until you've sent it that you realize it wasn't a good idea.

There's a popular Chinese proverb that says: "The best time to plant a tree was 20 years ago. The second best time is now." So when people ask us when the best time is to buy their first home or begin to invest in real estate, we always say now – as soon as possible. People sometimes say, "The crash is coming," as an excuse not to start investing in real estate. The truth is you can't catch a falling knife. It's not about timing the market, it's time in the market! Every day, you could come up with a new excuse if you allow yourself. You need to take the plunge today and if it's something that you're buying for the future, then just go for it. The market is going to go up and it's going to come down, but when you buy for the long term, the fluctuations don't matter as much since real estate investing isn't a get rich quick scheme.

In terms of getting your property as soon as possible, you will need to be beyond the probationary period in your job, show pay stubs and get a letter of employment. If you're self-employed, it's a little trickier. If you have a partner, one of you may need to get a job for a while to help with mortgage approval. Otherwise, you will need two years of tax returns to show your income. They'll average it out to calculate your earnings.

Even though you may not want to get a regular job, consider it your golden handcuffs. These golden handcuffs may mean you're in a job from nine to five, but it will help you acquire more properties. So instead of needing to get creative and look around for investors to carry a mortgage, you're able to use your employment to grow your assets.

Chapter 8

Empower Yourself

On social media, we get a lot of people asking if they can pick our brains. For some reason, there's a misconception that in a 30-minute consultation, you can come out with the mind of a real estate investor and be ready to execute.

In fact, we had a similar conversation with a software engineer. She already owned a property, had watched some YouTube videos and thought the missing piece was having a little time with us. We asked her if we could learn to become software engineers by having internet access and watching a few YouTube videos. She said it would take a year of learning on our own, or six months if we shadowed her and got mentored. This is the problem. There is a general misconception that since you don't need a degree to start real estate investing, you can just google it and come up with everything you need to be successful. This is why some people don't realize that the biggest investment is in learning from other people's experience, cutting the learning curve and getting personalized advice.

Not everybody's situation is the same. We wouldn't advise one student what we would do for another. We base it on their goals and needs. Unfortunately, we frequently notice people pretending to do better than they are or acting like they have a lot more experience than they really do. When it comes down to it, you find out they have a house they live in or investment property that is running at a loss. That said, don't be the person worried about chasing numbers. It's more important to make informed decisions.

We know that at this point, with all the information we've shared, you may be wondering if you're cut out for this. All the negative comments from friends and family aside, you may be telling yourself it's too complicated, you're not good with money, you feel like you're alone, it seems scary and you might be wondering if you can truly be successful with real estate investing.

This is exactly why we've built our community called 16WeekInvestor. It's a free Facebook group that you can join: https://www.facebook.com/groups/16weekinvestor/. Inside, we do live- streams, answer questions, talk about mindset, and give tips on how to be successful in real estate investing.

Trust us when we say we remember what it was like trying to navigate this on our own. That's also why we strongly encourage every investor to get a mentor to help them along the way. Not only can they help with specific situations, but they can also give their students confidence about their purchases.

So often immigrants and other people feel stuck in their jobs. They feel like there's no choice. Every day they get up and do this thing that takes up so much time in their lives. They don't even get to enjoy their time off. Then we get up and do the same thing again the next day. We want you to know there's a better way. You can be the creator of your life. The dreams you have of something better are all available to you.

It doesn't matter where you came from. It doesn't matter if English is your second language. It doesn't matter if you have a college degree. You just have to be willing to put in the work and push aside whatever thoughts are keeping you from starting. Again, if real estate investing is something you've been wanting to do, but you just don't have the support, please make sure you join our free Facebook group to get started.

Sometimes, as first time homebuyers and immigrants, we can easily be intimidated. It doesn't need to be this way. Remember you are the buyer of a property which means you are in a powerful position to say yes or no.

We had a realtor tell a buyer once they couldn't back out of an offer during the due diligence stage. This is totally untrue. We have to be able to stand our ground and know our rights. We need to be well-informed. We have the right to put in conditions on the purchase. We can request an inspection. If we're not satisfied with the results of the inspection, we can back out.

You always want to have something in your contract that allows you to back out of the deal. This may be an inspection clause, financing condition or as simple as spousal approval. It's okay if a deal doesn't work out. There will be other ones. If you're going to invest, you want to be sure about it. You don't want to have regrets about jumping into a deal without doing all your research, but you also want to avoid paralysis by analysis. This is another key reason to make sure you find a great realtor who isn't just out for themselves to get the sale.

About Working with Your Spouse

Sometimes people ask us what it's like to be married and be in business together. We do so much as a couple and make decisions for the family and business. Often, we feel like we are together 24/7 unless we decide not to go grocery shopping together.

We have learned along the way to find a balance between business and pleasure. It's not always rosy but we are in this together. We are united in our goals. We have gotten to a point where we can balance the two. In the beginning it was very hard. If there was a client that needed something and there was a personal issue, it would affect our business. It's all about understanding that there's a business and a personal side and being able to draw a line. It can be a mental line or a physical line.

Some people will clock out of their work at five o'clock and leave their frustrated feelings and emotions at the office. They then get to process on the commute home and vent to a supportive spouse on arrival. For us, that isn't an option as we work together and live together making it more important to always be open and honest about the way we feel. At times it can be challenging, but if you're able to express how you feel, acknowledge your partner's feelings then you can move on. We have realized that if we don't respect each other and honestly share how we feel about certain things, it's going to lead to arguing about something that's completely irrelevant down the line. It is a little hard to not be open and honest with each other when you are in the same space together for almost 24/7, so that's really been our biggest thing.

Chapter 9

Five Step Home Buying Summary

1. Get a pre-approval – you need to know what you qualify for before you start looking

If you want a high chance of closing on your house, check with your mortgage broker first. Nothing is more disappointing than having a realtor look for houses for you, then to find out you don't qualify. If you get the pre-approval before you go shopping, you'll know exactly how much house you can afford.

The reason you go to a mortgage broker rather than a bank is because the broker will shop around for you. Not only that, but you'll only have one credit check pull.

If you walk into the bank, it's only one bank. Every bank you go to will be a credit hit on your score. If you end up going to 10 banks, you've gotten 10 credit hits and it will have a negative impact on your credit score.

There's more on this in the Mortgage chapter.

2. Interview a realtor – at least three

When growing your team, we recommend you interview three realtors. This is to see what type of experience they have. Are they an investor, do they know the market and do they know the best areas to invest? They should be able to answer how the markets are doing right now and what the forecast is in two or three years? There are so many questions you can ask in order to get the right realtor to work for you. Then narrow it down to the realtor you feel will give you the best service for what you're looking for.

Check out Part 3 for more details on the exact interview questions to ask.

3. Start looking at properties – with the criteria you've given your realtor.

Your realtor will create an email blast with properties that fit your criteria, which also fit your budget. Then you let them know which properties you want to view. Hopefully, pretty soon, you'll have a property you want to put an offer on.

4. Put in an offer – negotiate the best deal to make your investment scenario work

You will negotiate through the realtor. This is also another reason why it's critical to get a realtor that will work for you and understands your needs and house criteria. Feel free to ask the realtor to provide you with a list of comparable properties and remember to put in your conditions. The realtor will then put together all the necessary paperwork to present the offer. Make sure you double check what's on that offer before you sign it.

5. Mortgage approval – fulfill all the conditions to get your financing

Once the offer has been accepted, your realtor will forward the documents to the mortgage lender who at time of approval may also have conditions. Generally, you allow ten to fourteen days for financing approval, inspection, and anything else you want to stipulate for your acceptance on the home.

When you're putting in these conditions, you're trying to protect yourself so when the day comes for you to remove conditions and move forward with the purchase, you feel 100 percent sure about your investment. If you're still feeling great about the property, you're good. You can go ahead. If you're not feeling certain about the property because you found an issue in the inspection report, you can back out.

First Time Homebuyer Mistakes
As a first time home buyer, it can be scary making a decision on what could be the biggest purchase in your life. Here are our top 10 list of common mistakes you can avoid so you can be a successful investor.

1: Bad Financing

2: Bad Location

3: Misjudging the Resale or the Rent Value

4: Underestimating the Expenses

5: Letting Emotions Drive Your Decisions

6: Thinking you will "Get Rich Quick!"

7: Doing Everything on Your Own

8: Overpaying for the property

9: Misjudging the cash flow

10: Not having an exit strategy

Here's a Bonus. Last, but not least, the most important is due diligence. In some cities, you may be tempted to make offers with fast closings, in as-is condition, and with no due diligence period. This may help you get a lower price, but for your first deal this is probably not the best route to go. Here are a few of the important things we usually do during our due diligence:
- Obtain a professional third party property inspection. If there are any repairs to be done, now is the time to bring in your handyman for estimates.
- Evaluate zoning and local ordinances
- Get a professional third party opinion of value and rental comparables

If you find that you made a bad assumption, you may need to renegotiate or walk away from the deal.
The reality is that if investing in real estate was easy, everybody would be doing it. Fortunately, many of the struggles that investors endure can be avoided with due diligence and proper planning before the contract is signed.

Part 3:
Real Estate
Investing 101

Chapter 10

Before You Invest in Real Estate

We were on a high after we played Cash Flow so we listed our place for sale. The house we were living in was a liability and not earning any money for us and that needed to change. We wanted to get an income-generating asset. We were so eager to start this investing journey that we started to look for our next house after about 30 days into our 90 day contract with our realtor. We put in three contingent offers on homes and all of them fell through because we were unable to sell our villa.

About 40 days in, our house still wasn't moving. Though discouraged, we persevered. We thought selling the house just wasn't meant to be as it was ss that we sabotaged the offers we received. On day 87, we got an offer that was just $3000 under asking then about a week before the contract was slated to end. Looking back, we see that we were self-sabotaging the sale. When our realtor would tell us that someone wanted to see the house, we thought, "Sure, we know how this works. They're going to come view the house and they're not going to take it."

It was hard not to lose interest in selling the house and that's exactly what happened. Eventually, we got so disenchanted with the process. Our realtor was so excited to get an offer which was so close to asking price but we declined. This prompted him to ask if we were serious about selling? Sadly, we had lost the vision, excitement, and the dream we found from playing the Cash Flow game.

Our realtor became confused and frustrated but we justified our response by sharing that we had nowhere to move to. Besides, we figured it would be another case of going back and forth and then having the offer fall through.

As luck would have it, our realtor came back with an offer at full asking. The buyer's only request was for us to leave the window coverings but, again we continued to sabotage the sale. We told him we would not leave the blinds secretly figuring it would kill the deal. In the meantime, we went through the motions of looking for the next house. We ended up going back to see a home we had initially seen on day 15 that we weren't sure of the first time around. Strangely enough, this time around, we could envision the suite, the kitchen, the bathroom and how it would all tie into a beautiful income suite. Our biggest problem was timing. We told the buyer we needed extra time, thinking this would be the next killer of the deal. Instead, the buyer agreed to everything we asked of him, even the potential extended time we would need to move out. Eventually, we couldn't come up with anything else to sabotage the sale.

At this point, we became quite content to proceed with the sale and started to look forward to the move. We thought it was smooth sailing from there. We had found a great house to move into and we had gotten what we wanted out of the house we were selling. But when we went to remove the conditions on the property we were buying, the bank told us they had overlooked something and would not be able to give us the mortgage after all. Once more, we were denied!

We now had to figure out a solution or risk being homeless. There weren't many mortgage brokers in our community but our realtor provided us with a referral which turned out to be our saving grace. Within 24 hours, she had a mortgage for us.

Could it be things lined up this way because we were meant to purchase this house? It had a private space upstairs which we could use for our office and other features we loved. Most importantly, we could rent part of it out to help us pay for the mortgage. This home would not be a liability like our last one. Our objective had been achieved.

Now, we can't say we grew up knowing we could be real estate investors like some kids grow up dreaming of being a soccer player, doctor or pilot. Becoming financially free through real estate investing has been a huge blessing to us. We understand what it's like to come from a background where we didn't have money. Now we want to educate and give back so others can grow their wealth in the same way. So many times we have these dreams in our heads of what we want to do or what we want to accomplish in life, but when we try to figure out how to make it happen, we end up with so many unanswered questions. The most common question we get is, "I don't have any money or how can I get into real estate without any money?" This is why there are people who think real estate investing is only for the elite. It's not. We want to show you how you can join us in being financially free.

There are some people who think getting involved in real estate is just about buying properties. What are the fundamentals? How do you know where to buy properties with the best returns? While growing your portfolio is important, it's more important to get the best returns. There is a right way and a wrong way to go about it and there are six important things you need to know before you invest in real estate.

1. Think like an Investor, Not a Landlord

To start your journey to wealth and financial freedom, your mindset needs to be that of an investor, not a landlord. Investors think like business people in terms of Return on Investment (ROI), cash flow, property appreciation, easy sale potential and more. Landlords just oversee properties and make sure the rent is collected and the property is kept up. When you think like an investor, you can invest anywhere in the world. You don't need to be or live there. When you think like a landlord, you may think you have to be close by in case something happens.

Let's talk briefly about property management. If we had a plumbing issue, we'd call a plumber. Does it matter where we're calling the plumber to? We had a leak from our hot water tank at our property in Cleveland while we were in Canada. We had to call a plumber to deal with the issue. However, if we were acting like landlords, we would think that we needed to be there to oversee it.

You also want to be cognizant of where you get more bang for your buck. We get a better ROI on our home in

Cleveland than some of our properties in other locations. That thinking lets us invest anywhere in the world with no limitations but building a great team. If you keep your focus on your goals, thinking like an investor, it's easy to find a way around any issue.

2. Location, Location, Location

It's important to research your location so that you know what you're looking for in a location so that you get a good ROI. You may think investing in a certain city seems great until you start digging deeper. Don't feel bad about changing your mind. This is your business so you need to make those tough decisions. Better to change your mind now than to find out later you made a rushed decision just to add an additional property to your portfolio.

You need to know:
- The rent values
- The rental demand for the specific city you're looking to invest in
- The economy - you want to invest in a diverse economy so that if one industry slows or shuts down your investment is not affected
- Why are people moving there?
- New jobs being created there
- The amenities there

Location also dictates your tenant profile. If you invest in rougher neighbourhoods, also called D neighbourhoods or the ghetto, you may have problems all the time. While there are people who have made money investing in these neighbourhoods, we believe there are so many other opportunities available so we have made a personal decision not to invest there.

We believe that you can invest anywhere in the world as long as you get a good ROI. Don't buy into the idea that you can or should only invest close to where you live. You'll limit yourself.

3. Non-Negotiable ROI

Once you find a property you like in a location of your choice, you need to know what your objectives are. What are you looking to get out of the property? Is it cashflow, a Return On Investment (ROI) or is it the one percent rule which means if you buy a property for one hundred thousand dollars, you want to get at least one percent of the purchase price in rental income? In this case, it will be $1000 in rent per month.

All calculations need to be done before you move forward in purchasing a property. We have a non-negotiable number. If we are not hitting that percentage or that number, we're not investing there. Our number is based on opportunity cost. If a property offers us a total ROI of 34% and we know we can't get that anywhere else, we make the purchase.

4. Create a Winning Team

If your desire is to eventually scale (grow) your real estate business, you have to create a team. Your team should consist of realtors, mortgage brokers, inspectors, accountants, trades and lawyers. You can also look to lighten your load with people like an administrator or property manager so you can create an empire in real estate.

We do not recommend trying to do everything yourself. You cannot be the person who does the cleaning and does the accounting. Then turn around and do the contracting work, mow the lawn, conduct the home inspections, change the light bulbs, and execute other duties. Even if you could, you should not use your time in this way. You need to build a team if you want to make sure your business grows and scales. Leverage other people's skills for those things so you can concentrate on the important parts of growing your business. Most of the time that's to acquire more great properties.

When growing your real estate business, you need a solid team. You need a realtor, mortgage broker, property manager, inspector, accountant, bookkeeper and lawyers. In some fields, it's not about getting just one of each team member. You need a team of trades; electricians, plumbers, handymen, cleaners and contractors. Make sure when you set out your business plan of investing in real estate you have included these people as business and life are team sports. Everyone has their specific role and specialty.

As part of our NMR (New Market Research), the first thing we do is join local real estate related Facebook groups. Through these groups and referrals, we connect with realtors and wholesalers. They'll start finding properties for us and conduct the initial analysis. Our next step is to review these leads by performing our calculations, market analysis and extensive research all prior to leaving our home. What's really great now is everything is online. It's an advantage as we can research any market and attend their online meetups. Just from this, we often feel like we are already in that city even though we are not (or even though we are still at home behind our computer screen.)

After all the research, it's now time to travel to the location to check it out in person, meet up with the people we've connected with online and network with other real estate investors. This gives us a bigger picture of how to go about conducting business in that city.

As our research continues, we interview the people we think would be great for our team. Our next addition is a property manager, (remember to interview 3 property managers before you hire one). Property managers are one of the most important members of your team as they will be managing your asset. It doesn't matter how good a deal you have, if you don't have the team to manage it. By contacting a property manager before you acquire the property, you'll have a better sense of the type of tenants and the manager's comfort level in managing in that neighbourhood.

When first exploring the Cleveland market, our realtor presented us with profitable deals which we were tempted to buy without consulting our team. During the due diligence stage, we provided our property manager with the three properties we were considering. Immediately, our property manager canceled two off the list. When asked why he did this, he stated the tenant profile was not ideal and if we chose to go ahead with the properties he would not be the one to manage them. Typically, if the property manager doesn't want to manage the property, that could be a sign it's not a good investment. We've walked away from deals that seemed good on paper, but when our property manager says, "I'm not going to manage it," we know it's not worth acquiring, no matter how good it looks. This could also be an indication you may have a hard time getting out of that property later as well. We followed his advice and are happy with our current purchase.

We started the same way when we were researching Phoenix. Prior to leaving, we researched the market and obtained a pre-approval to guide our realtor on our budget and spending capabilities. We used the first day to unwind as we were travelling with our one and three year olds. After that, we were doing 10 hour days looking at properties.

We take our time meeting and interviewing people who have been referred to us to ensure they are in alignment with our business goals and needs. We don't assume a referral means that person is great for us. It's important we conduct our due diligence and build a relationship with those people on our own.

When you build your team, understand that at times you'll have great people and at other times you won't. You may have to replace certain people or even the whole team, but it's all part of the process.

5. Have an Exit Strategy

Whenever you're buying a property, you should immediately think of your exit strategy. If your exit strategy is to sell, you need to know when you're going to sell and who you're going to sell to. Life is always changing. If you're living in the property, you might want something bigger. Think about who the next buyer will be. Could you refinance? Are you going to redevelop the lot? All these answers are things you need to consider when you are buying any property.

For example, you might start with suited homes, buying one house at a time. After that, you may want to get into duplexes and fourplexes. Eventually, you may want to buy apartment buildings. Maybe ultimately, you want to get into commercial buildings. You never know, but to do that, you might have to liquidate some of your smaller assets so you can get into those larger deals. You need to always have a plan of how you'll get out of every property you buy.

On the flip side, if you're not going to sell, are you going to redevelop the land? Are you going to build something else? What kind of property is your next purchase? What's your goal with all your properties? Who is going to be the end buyer later?

With a good exit strategy, you're able to start planning in advance. Many people will start in a single-family home and start growing their portfolio that way. As it grows, they'll save enough money to get into a multifamily. Know that when you're selling a single-family home, you have multiple options for exiting – selling to a homebuyer or an investor. When you're buying a multifamily, you're generally looking for an investor as your exit plan.

Too many people make the mistake of getting into a property and not thinking of what will happen down the line. This is a mistake that can set back some real estate investors. You need to ask yourself questions from the beginning. Am I going to sell? Will this be my retirement plan? Am I passing it down as an inheritance? If the latter, do I need to have conversations with future generations and ask what their intentions are? A while ago, we went to see a building that was part of an estate sale. Grandpa bought it and passed it down to his kids. They kept it as an investment for years and at their passing it was left for their niece. She had no interest in being in real estate and immediately sold it to the highest bidder.

6. Execution, Execution, Execution

"Plan your execution, execute your plan." Anonymous

Many people can imagine and dream of becoming successful real estate investors, but few will execute. Reading this book, joining our Facebook group or even getting mentored are all a good starting point, but do no good unless you are committed to taking action.

You must make plans that you are going to follow through with if you want to attain your goals. It's easy to imagine and fall in love with certain aspects of real estate investing: the desire, the excitement about the purchase, running the numbers, owning millions in properties, and changing lives. You can dream as much as you want, but if you don't put everything into practice and execute, you will not reach your dreams. Everything ends up becoming theoretical, however, executing the plan is what makes it all come together.

If you're worried that you don't have the resources to start investing in real estate, just concentrate on being resourceful and keep reading. We know a lot of people who have gotten into real estate with no money because they had the drive to succeed. They had the zeal necessary and they never gave up mentally. Some of these investors started with nothing and now own multi-millions in real estate, including resorts and commercial property. Anybody can do this as long as they put their mind and heart to it. Julian Hall sums it up perfectly, "Ideas are yesterday, execution is today and excellence will see you into tomorrow."

Chapter 11

The Basics of Real Estate Investing

As we get into the basics of becoming successful with real estate investing, we want to make sure you have a good overview of the process, steps involved, people you'll need on your team, and other necessary elements. We may touch upon concepts we've discussed previously but we do this so you can have the overall picture in one place.

You may be someone who is looking to buy your first property or you may be someone who is looking to grow your portfolio. Either way, we want to help you create the best portfolio for your specific goals.

According to Wikipedia, real estate investing involves the purchase, ownership, management, rental and or sale of real estate for profit. Improvement of real property as part of a real estate investment strategy is generally considered a subspecialty of real estate investing, called real estate development.

You may have heard people say you don't really own your home or other properties – the bank does. What we want you to understand is you control that asset. That's leverage and a strategy used for real estate investing. Don't think of the bank as your enemy like so many people do. When you work with the bank, you make the bank your business partner.

There are two ways to invest in real estate. One way is active investing and the other is passive investing. Active Investing is when you are a part of the day to day management of your   properties. You're hands-on or active in your business. When you invest passively, you may have a couple of properties or more. You might even just have one. No matter how many properties you have, you use a property manager to manage all of them for you. Then you collect your money every single month from your property manager. You're not active in the day to day operations of the rental property.

Many investors start out as active investors and then become passive investors. We remember when we started our real estate journey, we were very active. We were hands-on with the tenants. We interviewed them, completed the leases, collected rent, found contractors, etc. We were the property managers.

Some people are concerned because we hear, "Oh, I don't want to deal with a tenant issue at 3:00 a.m." That is the active part of real estate. But you have a choice. If you don't want to feel like you're trading your time for money, you can use a property manager to turn your role into a more passive role very easily. As we've mentioned before, in real estate, there's always an answer to every "problem."

There are other ways to be involved in real estate actively while you transition to be an investor. You could be a realtor, contractor, mortgage broker, or a property manager. All these professions and trades teach you valuable lessons. You'll learn about the market. You'll learn to evaluate and compare different types of properties. You'll learn to assess what homeowners and investors are looking for.

As a realtor, you may also get to see properties before they hit the market. Then you'll have access to incredible investment deals before anyone else even knows they exist. Is being a realtor a must in order to be an investor? The answer is no. We have partnered with realtors who specialize in working with investors.

For those who think they need a lot of money to get started in real estate this section is written especially for you. There are many ways to save up the money you need and get in for less cash than you thought possible.

1. House Hacking

One of the ways we accelerated setting aside money for our real estate investments is a concept called "House Hacking", which we talked about in detail in Part 2. This gives you a mortgage or rent helper so you're not paying the entire amount and can save your money instead.

2. Be a Landlord

A lot of people find themselves as landlords with their first property. Some do it on purpose and others become accidental landlords for many reasons including being relocated for work. When they buy a property in a different city, they can either sell or rent out their previous home. At times they can't sell their home but need a solution to avoid paying two mortgages, thus becoming accidental landlords.

3. Wholesaling

Some investors started their journey in real estate by wholesaling. Wholesaling has allowed investors with little capital to directly connect with home owners. An investor, Anna, was connected to a couple who needed to sell their slowly deteriorating home to retire. The home's (After Repair Value) ARV was $400,000. Anna negotiated a purchase price of $200,000 as the house needed $80,000 in renovations. Through her network, Anna assigned the purchase agreement to a flipper for $240,000 making Anna a $40,000 profit on that deal.

4. Lease Options

If you are unable to qualify for a mortgage, a good strategy to invest in real estate would be a lease option. A lease option will provide you the opportunity to secure a home today with the option to buy in three to five years or at the end of the lease period. This could be an advantage in markets where real estate values are ever increasing.

5. Agreement For Sale

An agreement for sale provides the buyer an opportunity to purchase a house at today's price without having to qualify for a mortgage. This is one of our favourite strategies as we grow our portfolio and are no longer in a position to qualify for a mortgage. It provides all the advantages of mortgage paydown and equity growth accumulation by the time you buy or sell the home.is bought or sold.

6. Sandwich Leasing

In a sandwich lease, an investor would rent a home from a landlord and subsequently rent it out to another party. With this strategy, investors are able to commit to a property with no money but need prior approval from the landlord to sublet.

7. 0% down payment a.k.a. Cashback Mortgages

When we were first introduced to investing in real estate with no money down, like many others we had our doubts. This strategy starts like any other owner occupied purchase, except at closing, the lender refunds your initial down payment. Depending on the bank you are working with, a cashback of two to seven percent would be returned.

8. Real Estate Investment Groups (REIGs)

A way to invest passively if you don't have a lot of money saved up is to participate in real estate investment groups. Like the stokvel concept we spoke about before, this is where a group of people with the same vision come together and agree to invest in real estate as a collaboration. We've been a part of groups like these where each participant puts in a portion of money that goes towards purchasing a property together.

Not everybody has the ability to jump into the landlord position right away or buy an entire property. So for those people who want to get started with less money, a real estate investment group may be the way to go. If you decide to go this route, make sure you do your due diligence on the group and how it is managed. At times the group is considered a corporation if it has been established and registered as such. That means if you are leading one, it's even more critical to make sure the proper reporting is being done. Leverage your team and have your accountant do your statements so you don't overwhelm yourself with it.

9. House Flipping

Some investors choose to flip houses to grow their capital.. You may have seen this strategy on TV where investors buy houses at wholesale prices and then renovate to sell for profit at retail. For example, you may buy a property for three hundred thousand dollars. You put in fifty thousand dollars in renovations. You then sell it for $450,000 to make a profit. This buy, renovate, then sell strategy is called "flipping".

Buy	$300,000
Renovate	$50,000
Sell	$450,000
Profit	$100,000 before taxes & expenses

When we started investing in Ohio, we could get a turn key (fully renovated) property for as little as fifty thousand dollars. Alternatively, we could buy a property that needed renovations for twenty thousand dollars and invest ten thousand dollars in updates. Once it was completed, the property would have a new value called the after repair value (ARV). With that new value we could refinance or sell the home. As an investor, your goal is to obtain an ARV higher than the total amount you invested to allow you to refinance and withdraw a portion of your investment. When refinancing, the bank allows you to withdraw 80% of the new value leaving 20% in the property as the downpayment and the bank's security. Typically when we refinance, we use those funds to grow our portfolio. If you decide to go this route, make sure you have the right team around you to execute the full strategy successfully.

10. Crowdfunding

This method raises small amounts of money from a large amount of people, typically online, to get capital for real estate investments. This way, you can invest in a wider portfolio without having to deal with mortgage requirements, real estate agents, tenant issues or contractors. The crowd fund manager takes care of all those day-to-day tasks to ensure the investors are happy. Thus, allowing you to gain the returns without all of the hassle of "fixing and flipping" homes on your own.

Now, we'd like to touch upon being a homeowner with an income suite as we did in Part 2. When you buy your first home, you may be excited and not want any tenants. Why is it important to have a basement suite (or an upper suite)? It's all about making money from your primary residence. We learned this on game night when we played Cash Flow. That shifted our minds. We were the ones paying for our mortgage and did not have a mortgage helper. Therefore, our house was a liability. As soon as we learned that, we knew we had to look for properties that had a mortgage helper .

Our goal was to make money with our property. That means if you already have a property, your next step might be finding a roommate and that's something you may need to get creative about. Do you have a basement space that could be converted into an income suite? Can you rent out your living room or couch? If you want to do a quick search on the MLS (Multiple Listing Service), you'll see that some of these properties are side by side duplexes where you can live in one unit while you rent out the other. Don't forget to run the numbers before you decide if this is the right next move.

If you don't have a property yet and want to make sure you can house hack it, work with your mortgage broker to find out how much you can qualify for. Then inform your realtor of your budget and he can do the appropriate search for you.

For the best results, be sure your realtor is aware of your intentions with the property, "I'm looking for something with a basement so I can convert it into an income suite." This will allow your realtor to narrow down the search to conforming (legal) suites. When buying suited homes, some investors prefer purchasing non-conforming / mother-in-law suites because they are more affordable as they have not been inspected and cleared by the city. You then have the option to legalize the unit which normally then increases the value. When purchasing a non-conforming suite, you run the risk of being shut down by the city since you can not legally have someone renting the basement as a separate unit. Some cities have operated this way for years, but keep in mind that this will be a risk you will be taking.

We will get into much more detail about the role of your mortgage broker in a subsequent chapter, but it's important to understand here that your mortgage broker is key to getting you financed. In a nutshell, your mortgage broker checks your credit and your financial status to determine how much you can afford.

Your credit score is a way for banks to evaluate the risk they're taking on giving you financing. Keeping your credit score up is crucial. We like to refer to good credit as the equivalent of having money in hand. If you don't have good credit, you are going to have a hard time with financing. Your goal should be to maintain a credit score above 700 as the rules continue to change. You are; however, able to qualify with a 650 credit score with some lenders and insurers at time of writing. A low credit score signifies to the bank the risk they will be taking on the loan and also shows how negligent one has been in the past. As a summary, the banks will rule this out as they will conclude they may not get their money back.

People with no Not having credit tends to have a hard time be quite challenging as the banks have nothing to judge you on. You'll need to build your credit with companies that will report your on-time payments to the credit bureaus. It may be difficult initially to qualify for a basic credit card and, if that's the case, you may need to explore prepaid options. When we started our investment career, we had our credit scores in the 500 range. We also share how we increased our score in a separate chapter.

When you let your mortgage broker know your intentions with your properties, they can also keep an ear out for different investment opportunities available to you. The reality is you don't know what you don't know. This is why you need a mortgage broker on your team who is knowledgeable and understands your vision on your team. We generally prefer working with mortgage brokers versus directly with banks as they are able to explore different lending options without multiple pulls on our credit which often leads to a lower score.

Some real estate investors are held back by their unwillingness to sacrifice their present comfort for future financial freedom. Having a clear vision and compass for the future is vital to one's success. Sure, it could be uncomfortable having roommates now, but knowing the money that you're saving is going towards getting your own home in the future can motivate you to stick through it.

We are often asked how we feel about short term rentals/Airbnb as an investment strategy. Our journey as Airbnb hosts began in 2014 when we were looking to increase our cash flow and generate as much income as possible to grow our portfolio. This quickly expanded from renting out one room to renting out over 10 rooms and generating $15,000/month. Over the last decade, a number of companies have been created with the sole purpose of investing in the short term rentals model. Some of these companies have generated millions in revenue in the rent to rent model. If corporations can do that, why can't individuals like us do the same? If you are not in a position to purchase a property, you could explore this model by either renting out a spare room or renting out an entire apartment to list as an Airbnb. Like any endeavour you consider, be sure to do your market research, notify your landlord of your intentions and check your city's bylaws.

While we do list through Airbnb, you need to decide if this is the strategy for you. As we've mentioned before, we don't give out blanket advice. We look at each of our students' unique situations to decide if a particular approach fits their goals. If you want to rent out your basement suite through Airbnb, it's definitely something you can consider. Again, be sure to check on your city bylaws and rules regarding short term rentals.

When doing our calculations, we generally look at a property as a long term rental first. If those numbers work, then we initiate research on generating additional cash flow through short term rentals. If you decide to get into Airbnb then change your mind later, be sure to look for a property that you can also rent to a full-time tenant and still make a profit.

If you're unsure about the area or whether you'll get a tenant, try a phantom ad. These are ads that help you research a marketplace. Place an ad with your anticipated rental rate and see if you get responses. Those responses will help you determine what type of area it is and the rent you can potentially get. Also do research on the crime rate, schools and what amenities are close by. This information is valuable especially if you're considering short term rentals.

If you're considering Airbnb, there's a link inside their platform where you can describe your property and Airbnb will give you an idea of how much the rates that hosts in your area with similar listings are making. Once you have an idea of how much you'll make, calculate all your costs to make sure the property will generate the income you expect. Some people buy based on emotions but if you don't do your numbers, it's going to cost you. Consider having a buffer and a reserve fund in place in the event things don't go according to plan so you can continue to cover your expenses.

Why are these calculations so important? Because cash is king. We don't recommend buying on emotion or speculation alone as there are too many variables. When we started in real estate, cash flow was always our intention. With a goal to replace our employment income and have options, we knew we needed to make smart investment choices. We needed to implement the BRICK technique. As we grew our business, we knew that for example five properties making $500 each in cash flow would generate $2500 every month. If we instead acquired ten of those, that would be $5000 per month. How much cash flow would it take to allow you to quit your job? Now determine how many properties that would be.

So many people don't realize their home is a liability. Even when we share this concept, they're not honest with themselves. Knowledge is power but the biggest power is when you implement. So now it's your turn to figure this out. Do you have an extra room in your house you could start using to generate income? Are you able to finance an investment property? Can you create an opportunity where you're renting a house and renting out the rooms? Can you rent out unused rooms in a house you're renting through Airbnb? You may be surprised with the amount of profit you can make.

You might be wondering, especially if you have a family, is it possible to have a basement income suite with young kids or toddlers? Yes, it's possible. We did it and you can do it, too. You can soundproof your income suite. With renting out a portion of your home, you get to determine the amount of space you're willing to give up. You get to decide how you create it or what you're looking for in a house that already has an income suite.

Every once in a while, we come across someone who would like to renovate a basement in a property they are renting. "Would it be crazy to renovate a basement in a house that I don't own?" Yes! Unless you have a purchase contract and an approval from the owner, don't do it. You would be increasing the value of someone else's property. What happens when the landlord chooses not to renew your lease? If you renovate the property and are paying the same amount of rent, they could turn around and let your lease expire and rent out to another party for more rent as the basement is now renovated.

If your plan is to purchase a property and then renovate it, that could be a good idea. If you are unable to qualify, there are creative options available once you conduct your due diligence and run your numbers. At that point, you can explore partnerships with someone who can get financing or you can do an Agreement of Sale as we mentioned in Chapter 7.

Another strategy investors recommend is properties near a University. Some investors will find a good student rental house and sign a five year lease with a tired landlord. With a long term lease that includes an ability to sublet, you can rent rooms to students and make extra income.

Real estate can be completely flexible depending where you are in your life and your goals. As we are looking to grow our portfolio, when buying properties, we go for the longest mortgage amortization length possible. With a twenty percent down payment, you can usually be approved for a 25 to 30 year mortgage. The longer the term, the more cash flow you'll make because the spread on your monthly expenses and what you're getting for rent is larger. Another reason to spread this term as long as possible is because you're looking at your properties as long term assets. You want to generate as much passive cash flow as possible today, letting your tenant pay your mortgage the whole time. There are times we advise students to double up and pay off their mortgage as soon as possible which aligns better with their goals.

Occasionally you can get tenants who continue to renew their lease and stay for an extended period of time. On several occasions, we met people who were content renting for years. Some had even stayed in the same place for 20years! As an investor, these tenants are ideal. As your tenant pays their rent, your mortgage and expenses are covered. During these years, your property will appreciate while also getting cash flow and the mortgage paydown. Long term tenants are wonderful. We love them since we don't have to keep searching for tenants. It's definitely one of the ways we enjoy growing our wealth.

Don't forget about your property taxes and your insurance when you're making your cash flow calculations. You don't want those extra expenses to affect your profit. We'll be talking more specifically about how to do those calculations in the next chapter.

As a recap, real estate investing is an amazing vehicle to create wealth. If you have a tenant, your tenant is paying down your mortgage. As time passes, your property will also go up in value. After 25 years as a rental, your house will be paid in full by someone else. At that point, you have options to do as you please with the property, including selling it.

Chapter 12

Real Estate Investing Profit Calculations

We really do love duplexes as investment homes. You don't need to worry about converting a basement or creating an income suite. You don't have to deal with roommates you may not get along with. You can have your own space and have a mortgage helper to expedite paying off your property.

As we have mentioned many times before, everyone's situation is different, so there's never a one-size-fits-all recommendation. If you want to get started in real estate investing, knowing your numbers is going to serve you well. Emotions can lead you to purchase a property that doesn't fit your requirements as you may end up buying a house that doesn't fit your needs or get you closer to your goals. Knowing how to calculate your cash flow is essential to your success.

On the next page is a sample of the calculation sheet we use when evaluating properties. To obtain a copy, please join our 16week investor group as one is available.

PROPERTY DETAILS
Address
Bedrooms/Baths
Square Feet
Year Built

GROSS RENTAL INCOME	Month		Year	
Current rent			$	-
Less: Vacancy Allowance	$	-	$	-
Net Rental Income	$	-	$	-
Plus: Other Income (Garage, Laundry, Parking)	$	-	$	-
Gross Operating Income	$	-	$	-
EXPENSES				
Property Management	$	-	$	-
Repairs & Maintenance			$	-
Condo Fees / Strata Fees / HOA			$	-
Advertising & Legal				
Insurance			$	-
Utilities				
Other Expenses: Cleaning, Snow removal, Landscapping				
Total Net Operating Expenses	$	-	$	-
Net Operating Income (NOI)	$	-	$	-
Debt Service				
Less Mortgage Payment	$	-	$	-
Less Property Taxes				
Total Debt Service				
Net Cashflow	$	-	$	-

MORTGAGE INFO

Total Loan Amount	$	-
Type of Loan		
Term (years)		
Interest Rate		
Down Payment		
Monthly Payment	$	-
Purchase Price		
Closing costs		
Rehab		
Total initial investment	$	-

Cash-on-Cash Return
(Annual before-tax cash flow (i.e., NOI)/Down payment)
Total ROI

Sample Property

Let's complete an example on a sample property.

You have a home you purchased for $349,000. Rents are the following: $1400 for the main floor unit, $1100 for the basement suite and the garage for $275. The total gross rent per month for this property is $2775.

Rent and Vacancy

The next step is to calculate the vacancy rate. This is done to account for the times the unit may be vacant. By deducting the vacancy rate from the gross rent, it allows for flexibility when your tenant leaves, so you have an allowance to cover the mortgage. In our example, we used a vacancy rate of three percent.

Property Taxes

The property taxes for the house in our example is $202 per month.

Insurance

The cost of insuring our sample home is $125 per month.

Utilities

In our example, the tenants will be paying for their own utilities. If you decide to include utilities for your units, be sure to account for that expense in the rent. If the rent is $2500, you would need to deduct funds to pay for the utilities. Ideally, you would want a house with separate utility meters. In the event you are like most single family home investors and don't have separate meters, a good rule of thumb is to allot 60% of the utilities to the tenants who live upstairs and 40% of the utilities to the downstairs tenants.

Repairs and Maintenance

Homes always have little things that need fixing. It may not come up every month but setting aside money for any future issues will help you be covered in case anything happens. We generally set aside five percent of the gross rent to cover this. If the furnace breaks or needs maintenance, you'll have this amount of money in contingency for you to use. Now you may be wondering how you determine a "safe" amount of money to set aside for repair and maintenance. Below we have included an image to assist in assessing the Lifespan of Things.[6]

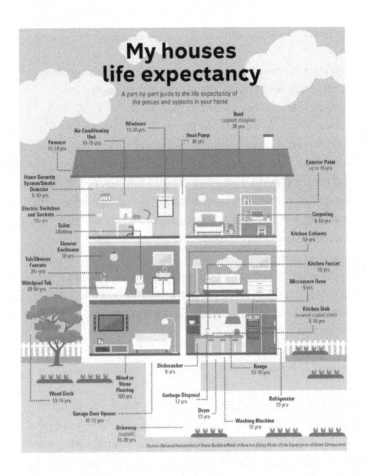

My houses life expectancy

A part-by-part guide to the life expectancy of the pieces and systems in your home

Roof (asphalt shingles) 20 yrs

Windows 15-30 yrs

Air-Conditioning Unit 10-15 yrs

Heat Pump 16 yrs

Furnace 15-18 yrs

Exterior Paint up to 15 yrs

Home Security System/Smoke Detector 5-10 yrs

Electric Switches and Sockets 10+ yrs

Toilet Lifetime

Carpeting 8-10 yrs

Kitchen Cabinets 50 yrs

Shower Enclosure 50 yrs

Kitchen Faucet 15 yrs

Tub/Shower Faucets 20+ yrs

Whirlpool Tub 20-50 yrs

Microwave Oven 9 yrs

Kitchen Sink (enamel-coated steel) 5-10 yrs

Wood or Stone Flooring 100 yrs

Dishwasher 9 yrs

Range 13-15 yrs

Wood Deck 10-15 yrs

Garbage Disposal 12 yrs

Refrigerator 13 yrs

Garage Door Opener 10-15 yrs

Dryer 13 yrs

Driveway (asphalt) 15-20 yrs

Washing Machine 10 yrs

Source: National Association of Home Builders/Bank of America Epoxy Study of Life Expectancy of Home Components

Property Management

Even when managing your own property, you want to set aside ten percent of the gross rent for property management. In our example that would be $250. The reason why you need to do that is because you are building a business. In a few months or years, you may not want to be self managing. You would want to outsource and most property managers charge ten percent. If you always account for this expense in your calculations, you won't have to make any adjustments as you will be accustomed to setting aside money for this item.

If you're self managing, you get to decide if you want to reinvest or save for that property or if you want to pay yourself. We tend to keep that extra ten percent as a contingency fund.

Tenant Gift Fund

You may be surprised to hear that we have a fund set aside for tenant gifts. This is a great way to stand out as a landlord since you want to create a good relationship with your tenants. In addition, you hope it encourages tenants to renew their lease if they're great tenants. We will usually provide a gift when a tenant first signs up for their lease, like a housewarming gift. We want to make them feel welcome in their new home. Other times we may give gifts on holidays like Thanksgiving or Christmas so they know we appreciate and care about them. The gifts don't have to be elaborate. A $25 Tim Hortons or a Best Buy card would suffice. Keep in mind the budget is 1% of the gross rent.

All the above are monthly expenses that must be correctly accounted for in order to calculate your total Return On Investment.

Net Operating Expenses and Net Operating Income

The Net Operating Expenses (NOE) is an important metric to determine if a property will be profitable. When you have multiple properties to compare, calculating these expenses makes your decision much easier. This can get a bit tedious, so inside our real estate investor program, we give our students a ready-made spreadsheet.

We have included the calculation chart that follows as a reference. To calculate the mortgage payments, we used the "Canadian Mortgage App". You will notice the total Loan Amount is $344,812 including Mortgage insurance. This amount is automatically charged on all mortgages with less than twenty percent down payments.

PROPERTY DETAILS

Address	123 Sample RD
Bedrooms/Baths	5/3
Square Feet	1425
Year Built	1977

GROSS RENTAL INCOME	Month		Year	
Current rent	$	2,500.00	$	30,000.00
Less: Vacancy Allowance 3%	$	75.00	$	1,500.00
Net Rental Income	$	2,425.00	$	28,500.00
Plus: Other Income (Garage, Laundry, Parking)	$	275.00	$	-
Gross Operating Income	**$**	**2,700.00**	**$**	**28,500.00**
EXPENSES				
Property Management 10%	$	250.00	$	3,000.00
Repairs & Maintenance 5%	$	125.00	$	1,500.00
Condo Fees / Strata Fees / HOA			$	-
Advertising & Legal 1%	$	25.00	$	300.00
Insurance	$	125.00	$	1,500.00
Utilities	$	-		
Other Expenses: Cleaning, Snow removal, Landscaping	$	-		
Total Net Operating Expenses	**$**	**525.00**	**$**	**6,300.00**
Net Operating Income (NOI)	**$**	**2,175.00**	**$**	**22,200.00**
Debt Service				
Less Mortgage Payment	$	1,458.45	$	17,501.40
Less Property Taxes	$	202.00		
Total Debt Service	$	1,660.45		
Net Cashflow	**$**	**514.55**	**$**	**4,698.60**

MORTGAGE INFO

Total Loan Amount	$	344,812
Type of Loan		Fixed
Term (years)		25
Interest Rate		1.99%
Down Payment	$	17,450
Monthly Payment	$	1,458.45
Purchase Price	$	349,000
Closing costs	$	2,000
Rehab		
Total initial investment	**$**	**351,000**
Cash-on-Cash Return		26.93%
(Annual cashflow/down payment)		
Total ROI		24.16%
(Annual cash flow/down payment + closing costs + renovations)		

Cash Required to Close

The cash required to close would be a combination of downpayment and in some cities land transfer tax. If you intend on updating your property or adding an income suite, be sure to include those costs here.

Inspection

Prior to buying this or any home, be sure you conduct a property inspection. This will cost approximately $550 to $1,000. Have this inspection as a condition of your offer. This is very important -- do not skip the building inspection. Conducting an inspection can help avoid costly surprises and fixes. In the event the inspection report reflects costly repairs, you can either renegotiate these repairs with the seller or back out of purchasing the home.

Closing Fees

In general, an appraisal is ordered by the bank but paid for by the buyer. The cost is between $350 and $600. Then there are legal fees of about $2000 in our example. The total closing fees is the money you need to set aside to acquire the home or the cash required to close.

Cash on Cash Return

The concept of cash on cash return is used to calculate the income earned on the cash invested in a property. This is considered one of the most important calculations in the real estate investing industry. It is calculated by dividing the Annual Cash Flow by the Total Cash Invested. In our previous example, it would be $4698,60 divided by the down payment of $17,450.00 and giving us the answer of 26.93 percent.

Think Like an Investor

I know at this point you might be thinking that $514.55 is not a lot of monthly income. You need to keep in mind that as an investor, we look for opportunities. In this example, we only needed a five percent down payment. We also wanted to share with you a minimum example so that you can see how it's still a profitable venture. What if you had multiple properties like this?

A lot of times as investors, we have to put a twenty percent down payment. With a higher down payment our cash flow and return expectations are higher. Keep in mind that a dollar today is going to be worth more in the future. If you can acquire and control a cash flowing asset that satisfies your goals today, you're in a better position tomorrow. Do consider if the interest rate goes up you are still able to generate cash flow, you just have to assess what your risk tolerance is.

Remember that cash is king. We shared a story earlier where we recommended that our student expedite paying off their house because cash for them meant irresponsible spending. If you feel that's you, there are multiple ways this can work. You can double up your payments, pay 15% of the purchase price yearly and pay an additional 10-15% monthly. Using this strategy, you could be mortgage free in under 10 years! Make sure to check with your mortgagor for their rules and regulations on this.

For those looking to expand their portfolio and grow rapidly, we recommend having liquid cash. Use it to buy more properties rather than rushing to pay off your mortgage. Keep in mind that as long as you have the cash flow and the property expenses are getting covered, with profit, you're still in a good financial standing. Again, everybody's situation is different, that's our disclaimer. If you want to be an investor, then you want to be able to leverage and do more than just one property at a time. In this case, paying off your house may not be the best strategy.

Chapter 13

Finding a Realtor

How do you find a realtor? How do you know if they are a good realtor? How do you find an investor focused realtor? In real estate, part of your success is about building a great team. The realtor is going to be one of the biggest pieces you need in this puzzle. They are the ones looking for the deals, sharing pocket listings, the listings that aren't on the market yet, and are the ones searching for properties that match your criteria.

There are so many realtors out there and you may be wondering how you can build a relationship with them and how to know who to work with? We have some standard questions we use to interview realtors in the cities we've determined are good for investment properties.

Always interview at least a minimum of three realtors. It's a bit like speed dating. You'll ask about specific things that will give you a bigger picture about their expertise and services. They will be helping to facilitate property purchases and sales which means they will be in charge of all your offer documents and any conditional clauses. They also need to know what to put in as conditions, how to read an inspection report, as a second set of eyes, and how to negotiate on your behalf.

Realtors help facilitate your purchase and make sure that you're protected as the buyer. You want to be in good hands. The last thing you want to do is try to experiment on your own and forget those clauses that need to be included and find out down the line that you missed something. Now you're legally committed to a binding contract that you can't back out of without consequence.

A good investment realtor will provide you with exclusive pocket listings that are not yet available on the MLS. They'll give you these before you even ask for them and they will prepare a comparative market analysis (CMA) on the house you're interested in. This will help establish the Fair Market Value (FMV) or After Repair Value (ARV) in investor terms.

You'll also want a realtor who can connect you with other service providers such as contractors and property inspectors. I remember when we first visited Cleveland, we didn't know anyone there until we connected with our realtor. He was able to do a comparative market analysis for us according to our strategy. Once he was able to find what we were looking for, he connected us with the team we needed.

The last thing your realtor will do is provide a competitive negotiation offer meaning they will negotiate on your behalf. You want someone who will look out for your best interests and work hard to get you the best deal.

When starting the interview phase, be transparent and let the realtors you talk to know you will be connecting with others but would like to see if they are a good fit. By doing that, you're laying the groundwork that this is an interview. Hopefully, this means they'll bring their best foot forward and they'll provide you with the most value, so you can make an informed decision.

Don't worry if some realtors refuse to answer your questions. Just move on to someone else. This is your due diligence and hard earned money that you're investing and relying on their expertise. If you don't know enough about the area, you need someone who is willing to educate and guide you in the right direction.

By conducting thorough online research, connecting with other investors in the area and conducting interviews with three realtors, you will become knowledgeable and more confident in your investment. What we're teaching you here is to save time for a good ROT (return on time). All you need is to align with great professionals who already have the knowledge.

We teach our students to use these specific questions to help them qualify real estate agents and ensure the property search aligns with their goals. Whether you're a first time homebuyer or a seasoned investor, these questions are the same.

Question 1: Are you full time in real estate?

This question is asked to determine a realtor's availability and to know if they will have competing priorities. We are not saying to avoid working with part-time realtors. Asking this question allows you to be better prepared and flexible in terms of how you will go about your business. You would also want to know what their hours of operation are and who would replace them if they were away.

A few months ago we were working with a realtor on selling our home. Soon after we found out she was expecting and due any moment. Our realtor was able to provide us with assurances that her office would be able to assist us during that transition period whenever she was unavailable. In the end, everything worked out as she had a plan in place.

Question 2: Which geographical areas do you serve?

If you have an idea of where you want to invest, you want to work with a local market expert. That's why we always ask how long a realtor has been in the industry. You'll connect with realtors who have been in the business for 20 years and others for only two years. You might end up working with the realtor with less experience as you may find they could be a better fit.

In our case, we already knew what we were looking for. We knew the type of property and area; however, we needed a buyers agent (purchasing realtor) to represent our interest. At times, when you work with experienced realtors, they might not give you as much time as you need. They have been in the industry for a while and have a busy client base. What we started doing was working with newer realtors. Through the interview questions, we found realtors with shared values and were able to create a win-win partnership.

Question 3: What is your experience and area of expertise in this industry?

Real estate agents need to be licensed in order to conduct business. You also want to know what experience they have and how it can serve you. Additional questions you can ask are: Do you focus on first time homebuyers? Do you work with investors? Do you specialize in condos, townhomes or duplexes? What is your area of expertise?

Question 4: Are you a real estate investor?

If yes, what type of real estate investments do you have? It is an asset having a realtor who is also an investor on your team as they are uniquely positioned to understand the market.

We once asked our realtor, "If you invest, why are you bringing us all these good deals and not investing in them yourself?" His answer was, "I can't take them all." This helped us understand the advantages of working with an investor-realtor so we knew they weren't just bringing the deals they didn't want.

Question 5: If I work with you, will I be expected to sign a buyer's agreement?

Remember this is all part of being upfront in the conversation. This is all part of knowing what to expect from each other so your realtor can best serve you. Some realtors will want you to sign a buyer's agreement as this will show your commitment to working with them. Don't feel pressured to sign anything at the start of the relationship.

Question 6: What is the median property price in the area? What are the average rental rates?

You want to know the average cost of properties in the area you're looking to buy in. Also find out the potential rental income you'll make.

You want to start doing your calculations once you identify potential properties that fit your criteria. When you look at these properties on the MLS and have all the information like property taxes, condo fees, etc., you'll have a better sense of the cashflow you could generate. When you calculate a property's potential in advance, you're in a better position to go see it and make an offer.

Question 7: Which investment strategies are working well right now in this market?

There are a lot of investment strategies available to investors. It would be an advantage to know what strategies are working in the market that you've chosen. If your strategy is to set up short term rentals, hearing all the challenges other investors have faced from the realtor could save you unexpected costs. A good realtor can help you pick the best strategy. They should be able to educate you on how the local market has been performing in the last six months and what they anticipate to occur in the next six months. That will give you the background of where the economy's going in that market so you can make an informed decision.

After speaking to three realtors, you are slowly becoming a local expert. You're learning about the market and researching what areas to avoid and where you could be more successful investing.

Your realtor can help evaluate investment properties and confirm the numbers provided by the seller during the transaction. It's critical to do your own numbers too.

We've noticed in the past where a seller will guestimate the costs associated with the property. The last thing you would want is to estimate taxes at $200 and they're really $400 or think that condo association fees are $150 and they're $700. These are discrepancies that could affect your cash flow. Always get the exact numbers and bills during the due diligence phase.

We once had a realtor inform us a home we purchased had a conforming suite. A few months after possession, our downstairs tenant called us as they had city authorities by their door. Turns out the neighbor had called the city as the basement suite was non-conforming. When asked about the suite, it wasn't enough to say our realtor had told us it was conforming. After a few long months, the suite was updated and ready for new tenants.

Question 8: Can an automatic search be set up to inform me of all new listings that are aligned with my investor profile?

It's good to get new listings right away so that you can do your calculations and see if the property is right for you. Keep in mind that your inbox may become flooded with listings. Make sure your realtor knows exactly what you're looking for to avoid feeling overwhelmed.

Question 9: Do you have access to pocket listings?

Pocket listings are those listings that have not hit the MLS yet. You want to be the first to know if a property is coming on the market. Ask your realtor if they have these listings and how you can get access to them. You'd be surprised to find out how many properties never hit the MLS before they're already sold.

Question 10: Are you familiar with commonly used real estate investing strategies, including double offer, red herring, vendor take backs and cash back at closing?

As an investor, you want to make sure that you're working with a team who understands your goals and will support you. When realtors know these technical terms, they generally also know how to present them to the seller. If you will be using these strategies, it's not enough that you know them and you're an expert on them. You also need to have a realtor who is knowledgeable on these terms as they may need to educate the other realtor on what to present to their client.

When we started investing in real estate, our realtor didn't know all of these terms. We had to educate her along the way. This wasn't ideal but worked well as we shared the same values and she was willing to learn. We made it work because we were educated and that's why we're bringing this up to you now so that you can decide for yourself.

Question 11: Can you introduce me to local contractors, property managers, etc.?

Most times we found our property inspectors through our realtors. Keep in mind we've also heard stories about how realtors are so influential with their property inspectors they end up letting things slip. You don't want this to happen. Inspectors have to mandate a certain level of service and have a code of ethics they must follow. Please do your due diligence even when referred by the realtors to local contractors.

Question 12: Is there anything else I should know about you, or working with your company, if we decide to proceed with this relationship?

It's important you are straightforward from the beginning. Set your intentions and let the realtor know what those intentions are from the start. Give the realtor an opportunity to tell you why exactly they think they're the best fit for you. Once they do, feel free to ask for references from investors or homebuyers they've worked with.

In summary, after you've interviewed three realtors, you are going to become the local market expert. You're also going to know what's upcoming in the neighbourhood and about the local diner that's a gem. This is information you could start sharing with your tenants and highlight on the rental ad.

Please also note if you've interviewed three realtors and you don't like any of them, you don't have to choose one.

Just continue interviewing, but minimally talk to three. Your biggest aspects to building your team is your realtor so don't just settle. This is time well spent.

If this all sounds like a lot of prep work before you even see a property, it is. You need to put in work to find the right realtor. Then you can get to the next steps of finding the right property, then doing the inspection, etc. There are so many stages that you have to go through before the acquisition of the property. If you decide that real estate investing is what you want to do, you need to be dedicated and put all your heart into it. Put all your mind into it because if you don't, that's when you fail and you'll be telling others that real estate investing doesn't work.

Chapter 14

Mortgages

Through the years, we've found out just how crucial it is to get the right mortgage broker on our team. No matter what city we want to purchase a property in, we make sure we have a knowledgeable mortgage broker on our side. If you need to get creative in your financing, this is also the member of your team that can help.

Credit Score Requirements for Homebuyers

Now more than ever, it's important to keep an eye on your credit score and know what affects it. Like we covered before, if you do not have at least a 650 credit score or a 680 credit score with Canadian Mortgage and Housing Corporation (CMHC), they will not approve your loan. In the instance where you have a couple looking to purchase a property, if one party's credit score slips down to 640 but the other is above 660, the application will be approved considering both parties are on the application. Only one party on the application needs a credit score above 650.

There was a time when the score requirement for some banks was as low as 600. Now, you could have a 640 score and not be approved for your home purchase. It doesn't matter how good your income is or how much downpayment you have.

There are Two Approvals in Mortgages

A principal point that a lot of people don't understand about mortgages is that when you apply for a mortgage, there are actually two approvals. One is from the bank itself and the other is from the mortgage insurance company. Not to be confused with homeowners insurance, mortgage insurance is insurance for your loan. The bank is the insured. With homeowners insurance, you are the one insured.

Unless both the bank and mortgage insurance company say yes, your deal isn't going to go through. Sometimes the bank will say no when the mortgage insurance company says yes. Then your job is to find another bank that will say yes. In some cases, if you have a good mortgage broker on your side fighting your case, they can convince the bank to change their mind. As well, the bank could say yes and the mortgage insurance company says no.

In the case where you're putting down 20% or more, you don't have to get mortgage insurance but many times our students conserve their down payment money to buy more properties instead of using it all on one home. In this case, with a five percent down payment, mortgage insurance would be required provided this will be an owner occupied unit.

Proof of Down Payment Cash

There are two items that the bank is going to want when making a request for financing. First, they're going to ask about the amount of cash you have available. The typical minimum here in Canada is five percent for owner occupied units. Second, they'll ask where the funds are coming from and you will need documents to prove it. If you say, "I've saved up in my checking account," then the bank is going to want to verify that with three months of bank statements. This will prove the legitimacy of the funds and show that the money has been saved over time. If they see a recent $30,000 deposit into your bank account, they will question where it came from. Legitimate answers are things like: I just sold my home, a car, or I just got a bonus from work. Those things are reasonable, but then you will also be asked to prove it with a bill of sale, registration, the T4 slip, or your paystub.

There are some mortgage brokers who can hold an interest rate for 12 months, so you could get pre-approved up to a year in advance for your home purchase. At that point though, you would likely need to re-submit documents to prove your credit score, job status, and cash reserves.

Two Big Impacts to Your Credit Score

There are two major credit companies in Canada. One is called TransUnion and the other is called Equifax. The Equifax system is connected to the borrowell.com website where you can get a free credit report. For safety and security reasons, you often want to guard and track your credit score as there are no costs associated with this search.

TransUnion reports to creditkarma.ca. Make sure to check what's on this site so that there are no surprises with your score either. The worst thing is to find the best house at the best price and then learn that your cell phone company dinged you with a late payment in the middle of a real estate deal.

The first big impact to your credit score is how much credit you have available versus how much you owe. Maybe you've heard people advise you not to max out your credit card. You will actually get a better credit score if you increase the limit because you keep using what you always use. For example, if you have a $5,000 credit card limit and use $4500 monthly, that's bad for you because every month, you're maxed out. They'll see that even though you pay it off monthly, you will max it out again.

So the biggest recommendation in this case is to get a $10,000 limit then only use $4000 or $5000. Then you're only using half of what's available so your percent usage is lower. In some cases, just getting a bigger credit limit will boost your credit score.

The second big impact to your credit score is who's been looking at your credit and how many times your credit is pulled. If you are shopping for mortgages, our recommendation is that you deal with one broker so they can do one credit check and then be good for all the banks that they shop your deal to. The worst thing is to go to 10 mortgage brokers and get 10 quotes and 10 credit checks.

If, for some reason, you do shop at multiple banks or brokers, three checks in one month would be the maximum credit checks you would want to do. Watch out for websites that are posting low interest rates just to get you to click and enter your information. There's usually a fine print there that disqualifies you from that loan or puts extra parameters, like additional down payment or paying for points, in order to get you that rate. So please, buyer beware in these instances.

Income Versus Expenses

You will always be asked on a mortgage application how much you make and how much you owe. Don't hope that the bank won't find out about your car payment or any other expenses. It's best to be honest because if you can't be honest on the application form, your broker will find out when they pull your score and may lose trust in you.

A job letter, a pay stub and typically two years of T4s, to show that you've been consistently making a certain level of income are needed for your application. If you've just started your job, you will be required to get past your first three to six months of probation before you can buy your home.

On the other hand, if you run your own business, the bank will want to see how much your business makes versus how much you're paying yourself. In some cases, there are people who make thousands in their business, but they only pay themselves $30,000 a year. Even though you can prove to the bank that your corporation makes thousands, the bank is still not going to approve your mortgage.

That means if you're a business owner, some pre-planning is essential. If you increase your taxable income, you may finally be able to buy that home that you always wanted. Alternatively as a sole proprietor you would need to be in business for two years. For those who are self employed, you're either going to pay the banks or you're going to pay the tax man, so plan it out so that you can get what you want.

Gifted Funds

There are rules specific to different mortgage programs as to how gifted funds can be used. You have to fit the program's rules. If you have a high credit score over 700, you can potentially use funds from a line of credit. If you don't have a high score, then you can generally only receive monetary gifts from your immediate family. Typically, most banks just have a letter or a standard form that says something to the effect of, "I'm giving this money to my child and they don't ever have to pay me back if they don't want to." Not all banks allow monetary gifts so if you know you're going to use gifted funds, make sure your bank accepts them.

Strategies for Real Estate Investors

As an investor, you'll want to keep a strong income and expense column. Cash flow is king. What kind of rents will you get? What are the mortgage requirements? Every mortgage you apply for as a real estate investor needs to have the lowest possible payment option. Even if a student says, "My goal is to buy one house and pay it off in five years," we still recommend the lowest possible payment. If you're putting 20% down, get a 30 year mortgage.

In some cases, variable mortgages rates may be lower than fixed. Today, there's not a huge difference so we recommend fixed rates if the property is a buy and hold for a long time. Choosing the right interest rate, the right product, and getting a long amortization is key for real estate investors for a higher cash flow. Sometimes you can take one of your properties that you've had for a long time and reset the amortization. That means you'll restart back to a 30 year mortgage, thereby lowering your monthly payment. Instantly, your cash flow looks great to a bank and they'll approve you for another property.

Another important element of real estate investing is to take the emotions out of it. Don't make your financial decisions based on fear or greed. If you think, "If I don't buy this, I'm going to miss out," you may make a decision on a property that may not be right for you. Later on, you will have regrets.

There always needs to be a plan. Know where you're going and how you're going to get there. Ask yourself, "How big do I want this business to be?" Do you want to buy 100 properties and go really big or do you want to buy five properties, pay them all off and retire with really good extra income? No matter what you choose, it's never wrong but you do need to know what you want so that you can intentionally aim to get there.

Then it's really easy where you're faced with a choice between two properties. Is this property going to get me closer to my financial goals? It ends up clear and you don't have to guess.

When to Go with a B Lender

The simple answer of when to go with a B lender is when the A banks are starting to say no. A lenders lend to those with great credit and they give them the lowest rates. B lenders help those who have imperfect credit or may be over extended. The risk for a B lender is higher, so the interest rate you'll get is also higher. A B lender will likely also ask for a larger down payment to mitigate their risk. If deciding between purchasing a property or not, the B lenders makes the most sense. Pay a little bit higher interest rate and purchase the property.

If you don't have the down payment, that's different. Most times you will run out of down payment money before you exhaust all your mortgage and lending options. So B lenders are definitely part of that growth strategy, but we don't recommend using them right away. If your cash flow is not strong the A banks will soon turn you anyway. The B banks are more flexible, so you can use them after you are maxed out on A bank loans. Your mortgage broker, if you have a knowledgeable one, will know which A banks to use when and where.

Porting a Mortgage

Porting a mortgage means you're transferring your current mortgage from one property to another. For example, let's say I relocate and have to sell my home that has a mortgage on it. Porting it means I can transfer that mortgage to my new house. So instead of paying back the mortgage contract or breaking the contract and potentially getting charged a lot of money, I'm going to port it and bring it with me to the new house that I buy.

To port a mortgage, you're still going to go through the same checks and balances that anyone would for a new mortgage. The only real benefit is if your mortgage interest rate is lower. If your mortgage is two percent and all mortgages today are at three percent, the advantage is that you have part of your mortgage on the new house at the lower rate of two percent. In the scenario where you're buying a bigger home and you might not have enough mortgage on your current mortgage, you may have to top it up with an extra mortgage or three percent. So they will blend the two together and come up with an interest rate that's somewhere in between.

Note: for those people who may not know, in Canada, a ruling came out effective July 1, 2020. The government is cutting back and the fancy terminology is GDS. In layman's terms, what it says is that the mortgage payment for your house can only be a certain percentage of how much money you make. Now, we can't buy the same price point of a house that we could before the changes. This ruling created a nine to 13% reduction in what you can buy. So at 10 percent, if you could buy a $450,000 house before, now you can only afford $405,000. That's $45,000 less.

Chapter 15

Our Biggest Lessons While Learning on the Job

One of the reasons we feel mentors and coaches are imperative is because they can share their lessons so you can get to success faster. We feel some of the best ways we can teach you about real estate is just to share our stories and experiences. There is an unlimited number of combinations and factors that could happen in just one purchase, you just can't predict what could happen. But you can be prepared to work through anything that gets thrown at you.

While we could try to just say, "Do this," and "Don't do that," there's not as much impact as hearing from our journey. These next stories share exactly what it was like to be in the trenches of some of our first purchases. We never look back at these stories with any sort of bitterness. Instead we use them to illustrate over and over again that some lessons can only be learned on the job. Every property purchase is unique and tenants are as unique as there are people in the world.

The Rental Board and The Residential Tenancies Act

At the start of our real estate journey, we had a tenant who wanted to get out of her lease before it was over. She told us she had found a better place and she was ready to move out. Although we went back and forth trying to get her to stay, she was very adamant that she wanted to leave. In the end, we felt like there was nothing we could do.

The surprise came later when she demanded to get her damage deposit back. At which point we informed her she had left early from her lease and we had not found someone to replace her, therefore we kept her damage deposit. However, she shared that since we hadn't done an entrance and exit inspection with her, according to the rental board, she was entitled to get her deposit back.

We had no idea there was such a thing as a rental board, but we came to learn there's one in every city. The rental board regulates the renting in a city. Once we realized this was a real thing, we did our research, contacted the board and found out she was indeed correct. Because we did not conduct an entrance inspection and we therefore could not do the exit inspection, we owed her the damage deposit. At that point we were forced to refund her damage deposit.

Luckily, we were able to rent out her space the next month, but the lesson we learned was to make sure we did those entrance and exit inspections and to check with each city where we had properties so we knew the rules. Every city has a rental board and they're the governing party for landlords and tenants. They help mediate any issues and it's supposed to be a neutral board to help both sides. If you're looking for the rental board in a city where you want to buy properties, a simple Google search will give you the contact information you need.

The rental board also known as The Landlord and Tenant Board is operated by a city's government to provide dispute resolutions between landlords and tenants. The rental board is also in charge of making rental rules in their city. We make sure we learn what the Residential Tenancies Act says in every city we have properties in. To make things easy, we will use the rental agreement form they provide so that we know we are following the rules and using the language they prefer.

Another tip we learned is when we call the rental board, never call as the landlord. You always want to call as the tenant because even though they are supposed to be a neutral party, they seem to give you a biased opinion. At least that's been the way it has been for us whenever we've needed to use them. Instead, I want to call as a tenant and I want to say exactly what my tenants will say. Then I will know what advice they would give my tenant if they call. Usually they'll advise the tenants of their rights, even point them to the exact section or part of the Residential Tenancies Act they need. We believe they may have more sympathy for the tenant in most cases since, as a landlord, you are considered a shark.

Renting to Groups of Friends

One of our three bedroom units was available and we rented it out to a group of three friends. At the beginning everything was going well, we assumed they were following the rules. One day, we went to check on the unit and found a pet. Our rules clearly stated no pets and no smoking. We reminded them of the no pet policy to which they tried to claim the pet was their friend's. We then notified them they needed to pay extra to keep their pet.

During that time, we had a tenant in the basement who would complain about their loud parties that would last until 2:00 a.m. We spoke to the group many times about the issue until they finally decided to leave. During the move out inspection, we identified damages to the unit which the tenants had tried to cover with paint and mudding. We learned from this experience then that you have to interview all parties who will be living in the house when you rent to a group of friends.

Here we were thinking we had checked all the boxes and mastered the entrance and exit inspections, and we had a different problem with a group of friends not following the contract. It was so overwhelming to deal with them we started wondering if this was the business we truly wanted to be in. In fact, we found out they were also smoking in the house.

At the end of their lease, which we didn't renew, we conducted the entrance and exit inspection report in the 10 days window according to the rules of the local Tenancy Board. At the end of the inspection, a statement of accounts and all deductions were submitted to break down any deductions that were taken off the damage deposit. Upon receiving it, the tenants disputed the claims. After 6 months of having moved out, they filed a claim with supporting photos and documents showing their entire damage deposit was used up in fixing the property.

Since they had already been so argumentative, it was no surprise that they had filed a claim. When we ended up at the hearing, we believed it would be best for the adjudicator to hear both sides in their entirety – if we couldn't agree, the next step would be to go to court. Both sides shared their evidence and we had our rebuttals until it was done. At the end of that, we stated that according to the Act, the tenants had six months to file a claim or the statute of limitation would be exceeded and it was month eight. The adjudicator sided with us and we got to keep the damage deposit in its entirety.

Sometimes Tenants Lie

One of our Airbnb rentals was booked by a group of medical students doing an internship for six months. We suspected their internship was cancelled, but that's all speculation. After enjoying a 40-day stay at our place, they sent a message stating there were bed bugs in the house. So obviously as an out of state or out of country investor and landlord we started thinking of all possible scenarios and costs that could be associated with this. With a quick Google search, we found out how seriously Airbnb dealt with bed bugs. A possible shutdown would occur and all your bookings would be canceled for as long as three months. When we found that out, we were in a panic.

We knew we needed to gather more evidence so we asked them to send us pictures and videos. Airbnb was then involved and requested photos of bite marks. It was interesting that every time we asked for evidence, it took the guests at least 24 hours to provide it. We started to get suspicious.

Airbnb knows that issues can come up so they have a process where the guests and hosts can communicate via the platform. We had received the message from the guests on Monday and we responded with an apology, suggesting they pack up and leave so we can rectify the situation. But their response was they couldn't leave right away. They wanted to leave on Friday because that was when their internship was ending. This only caused us to be even more suspicious as we failed to understand why someone would want to stay in a place infested with bed bugs? It didn't make sense.

We insisted they leave as the place was unsafe. Interestingly enough, they responded by saying that they would close the door to the specific room, wash the bedding and do some cleaning. When the time to dispute the contract fees with Airbnb came, we pointed out that if you're calling on Monday paranoid and worried about bed bugs, but want to wait to leave until Friday, why not stay until the end of your term?

Typically Airbnb tends to side with guests, but this time they were able to see that this may have been fabricated. However, they also have to take a stance of being fair adjudicators so they only charged for the nights our guests were there, but allowed us to rent out the house immediately after, which rarely happens in these types of cases.

We wanted to be certain our next guests would have no issues, so we took it upon ourselves to block our bookings for three days while we got an inspector to evaluate the place. Their feedback was that there were no significant signs of bed bugs. The inspector suspected the guests moved in with them in transition. We exterminated the entire house for added peace of mind. In the end, we had to refund the guests $2,000 for an issue they caused.

Cash For Keys

We find most of our tenants through online and social media advertising. We screen for employment and references. When looking for tenants in a shared accommodation, we ask a lot more lifestyle related questions to better match roommates.

Through one tenant who was struggling to pay the full damage deposit as we requested, we learned that it could be spread out over three months. A few months after moving into the house, the tenant started to be late with his rent and referring us to the Rental Tenancies Act. Previously, we rented out based on mutual trust and respect and hadn't experienced a professional tenant. When we did, we realized he had numerous cases with the rental board and had we done more research before we approved his application, it would not have been approved. For privacy reasons, this option is no longer available in some cities, but it's worth looking into if you can.

With this tenant, there were several lessons. What we learned was you should always call more than one landlord. We learned that his previous landlord provided a glowing review in order to get him out of his house. Be sure to call three or four landlords or character references prior.

By the fourth month, we were having a lot of challenges with the tenant sleeping on the couch blocking the only TV in a shared space. He had even moved the blankets from his room and claimed the couch as his bed. His rent was constantly paid in full with penalties but late. He was working full time but had mastered the system as he decided to stop all rent payments by the sixth month. At that point, we decided to ask him to leave, to which he refused.

The road to eviction is a lengthy one. To start this process, tenants must be served with a written notice that states reasons for evictions and when their tenancy is to end - which they can dispute unless it's due to unpaid rent. In the event they do not leave, the landlord has 10 days after the tenancy ends to file an application with the rental board. Depending on the case volumes, this process could take a month or two before your hearing. Once a judgement is made and the tenant still refuses to leave, an eviction order must be filed and that process could take a month. Before you know, the tenant has been there for three months without paying any rent. Our hands were tied.

Knowing that process, the tenant started to feel and act like "the boss" and be disrespectful and made other tenants feel uncomfortable. One tenant provided notice and said she was leaving if he stayed. After reading his case files, we realized he was a professional rent-free tenant. He knew his rights and knew he could stay without paying rent for a certain period of time. While talking to other landlords about this, we learned of a concept called "cash for keys" where you pay the tenant to turn the keys in and leave. We were hoping this would work and get him out.

When we approached our tenant, he was already a month behind in rent. On top of living there rent free for that time, his demands included a $1,000 payout and the TV that was recently purchased and placed in his room to move him from the couch. He also insisted on getting his full damage deposit back as well. This guy was truly a professional who had done this many times over. We reluctantly agreed as we felt we were being held hostage. As he started "looking" for a place to move into, he stated there were no options. We assigned staff to help him find another place to rent. In exchange, he agreed to move out at the end of the month where we would exchange a cheque for the keys.

We were astonished at the confidence this tenant could have being a month behind in rent and making demands including being paid to leave. At the time we had all intentions to pay him out, but as we continued to do our research, we found out he was aware of this strategy and had used it a few times prior. We were very upset. We toyed with the idea of putting a stop order on the check. We advise all our students to not let their tenants know they are also the owner of the property. Our tenant believed we were the property managers. After a few days deliberating on this, the tenant returned with one more demand, he wanted a certified check. We replied the owners were unavailable and unable to obtain one. His options were to either take the check as is or return at a later date for a certified check. He was desperate so he took the check and the television as he returned our keys for a smooth departure at 4pm.

We immediately changed the locks but to our surprise he returned 3 hours later since he felt the day wasn't over and was entitled to access the place until midnight. He was furious he was unable to get in so he damaged the lock. Soon after, he called demanding access, mad that the locks had been changed, swearing at us. We reminded him that he had checked out and an exit inspection had already been conducted. Additionally he hadn't paid rent for the month he was demanding to complete in the house. As we returned to the house, we realized the lock had been damaged to a point we couldn't get back inside and needed to call a locksmith to change the locks again.

Three weeks later, the tenant was notified by the bank the check had bounced. He called us furious as he exclaimed he had taken a cash advance so now the bank was asking for their money back. He called every day threatening us. He then called the police and insisted he was locked out of the house and he still lived there. He would also randomly show up at the house. Eventually we filed a restraining order as he was stalking us around town. When discussing these issues with the police, they smirked as they stated he was known to them because of the issues he had caused in the past. The tenant went on to file a case with the rental board claiming we refused to return his damage deposit, wanting to also charge us for the NSF and other fees. The adjudicator quickly dismissed the case as she called it extortion and we all decided to put it behind us and move on.

During this time, we were still looking at properties and trying to keep a positive outlook on real estate. We already had a few doors, but we were questioning the future of this business. It wasn't that we didn't want to continue; we decided what we needed to do was to re-strategize. We had a two year old and a new baby at the time so we took a step back to reevaluate why we were doing this -- we needed to reconnect to our why.

Our initial "why" was to achieve financial freedom and be home with our son. We now had that financial freedom. Colleen had already quit her job. We were traveling. Why did we need to do this? What were we hoping to get out of it? Did we really need to buy more properties? The answer was a resounding yes. We just needed a new "why". We also knew we had to do more to make ourselves feel comfortable with our investments like putting temporary external security cameras on certain units and for new tenants doing more research and conducting better background checks so this kind of situation wouldn't happen again. We realized how important doing our due diligence was.

If you're getting into real estate make sure you ask the right questions. Why are you investing in real estate? What are you hoping to get out of it? Are you looking to get yourself out of debt? What kind of property do you want?

The problem was never real estate investing. The problem was not asking all the right questions, partially doing our due diligence and looking to learn on the job.

Chapter 16

Five Ways to Repair Credit

When we bought our first property almost a decade ago, we were so excited. We had worked so hard and waited for so long. If you remember, it took us two years to save up enough money and we happily went to our mortgage broker. Imagine how discouraged we felt when we found out we were not approved.

Our hearts sunk. This was the moment we had worked six jobs between us to be told our credit wasn't good enough. We hadn't even heard about credit before or how to check or monitor it. We knew we needed a crash course in credit repair to pursue our goals.

This is what we learned about how you can improve your credit:

1. **Pay Your Bills on Time**

This may sound elementary to many people but for us, we had no idea how important this was. Creditors, mortgage companies and banks want to be confident they're lending money to someone who will pay them back on time, so they will look at your past history.

Zeb
Many times I would pull money out and not be consistent in the repayment terms. I didn't pay it back within 21 days.

Sometimes I would skip three months here and there or even five to six months because I had no idea what I was doing.

Paying your bills on time is about 35% of your credit score.

2. Lower Your Credit Utilization Ratio

Credit companies will calculate what they call a Credit Utilization Ratio. This is how much of your credit you are using versus your available credit limit. Keeping the amount of credit you're using (the "utilization") to 25% or lower of your overall available funds helps to improve your score. Creditors see a low utilization ratio as being responsible.

3. Pay More than Your Minimum Payment

If you're using a card that is charging you interest, the minimum payment is generally interest only, so it's to your benefit to pay more than the minimum required, otherwise you will be hard pressed to ever pay it off. If you pay more than the minimum payment, you'll be paying down principle and be able to pay off your card early.

4. Do Not Open Numerous Credit Card Accounts

When you continually apply for new cards or apply for five or ten cards in a month, you will get multiple hits on your credit score and it will indicate that you're desperate for credit. Lenders will think that you don't have money or that you're just trying to live off credit, and you don't have the money to pay them back.

5. Make Sure You have a Clean Credit Report

A clean credit report means that you don't have any negative comments or delinquent payments. It also means that it is free of mistakes. Our credit was good after a year of paying on time, lowering our utilization and watching how we were applying for credit. For some people, it won't take as long to get a clean credit report and for others, it may take a while, especially if you've had a bankruptcy or your account has gone to collections in the past.

6. Check Your Credit Report

It is important that you regularly check what's on your credit report because it's not always right. Catch those mistakes as early as possible so it won't affect your score and if you do find an error, you can contact the reporting agency with proof of why it's wrong to get it rectified. You can request your report directly from the reporting agencies or use services like Credit Karma or Borrowell.

If you're going to use credit cards, please make sure you are responsible with them. Otherwise, you can get into a lot of trouble pretty quickly. Credit cards are not right for everybody. When we started investing in real estate, we were using our credit cards and considered the bank our joint venture partners. On occasion, if it made sense, we would use our credit cards for down payments on properties. This can be a very risky endeavor for some people.

Being an immigrant, we didn't always have the normal options available to use so we took calculated risks. At times, you may also feel the need to support family or help someone out back home and can't ask mom or dad for money especially if they also need your help.

What's really great is we discovered some credit cards would allow you to convert them into a line of credit. If you've been responsible, you can also call your bank to see if they'll increase the line of credit on your card. Every six months we set a reminder on our calendar to call the credit card company to see if there was an increase available and then took it. When we got to the limit of our increase, we then converted the credit card to a line of credit which gave us lower interest. Another thing we do when the credit card interest gets high is that we would negotiate with the bank to get a lower interest card. So instead of being at 19.99 percent, we now had the bank as a private lender at 11% interest.

Chapter 17

How Fast Do You Want to Go?

Much like our title, "You Can't Save Your Way to Wealth", indicates, it can be a tough and slow road to saving money from your job alone. If you remember our story about getting denied at the bank, even with $12,000 in hand, you know that it took a lot of dedication to save up that amount from our jobs and we had three jobs each! We knew that we couldn't afford to give up though. We weren't going to settle with staying in the rat race.

There were definitely a lot of choices on what we could've done with that $12,000 and, honestly, it felt like we should get rewarded for our hard work. Blowing it sounded like a lot of fun but it would've been temporary happiness. We wanted a lifetime of freedom to do those things that made us happy, so we chose our future rather than immediate gratification.

Zeb

When we look back on it, what happened next was really an accident. I was already having issues with the driving school that I was working at as I got laid off. A few months prior, my in-laws had already suggested, "Why don't you start your own driving school?" So, it was really our future lining up for us when the driving school called asking me to bring in my keys and take my last cheque.

Again, if you recall the story, we ended up opening a driving school and buying our driving school vehicle with that $12,000. It wasn't something that we planned. We had people asking for driving lessons, but due to my moral compass, I couldn't teach them on the side. All of the sudden, I was free to do exactly what I was being asked and build a business with it.

The driving school business was all about seeing an opportunity and filling a need. While I was being employed by someone else, I couldn't fulfill a need in our city. There was only one driving school at the time and it was owned by an older couple who hadn't changed anything about the way they were doing business from the time they opened it.

So we became the second driving school in town. We purchased our first vehicle in cash because our credit was still bad, but even though we had some old students asking for lessons, it wasn't smooth sailing from there. Our competitor started to badmouth us, spreading rumors that we weren't officially licensed. People became unsure of us. We got to the point that we had to drive around with our official certificate hanging in the car.

The business idea really came from what we had learned from "Rich Dad Poor Dad". We were navigating our way through the cashflow quadrant. When we both started as employees, we thought we could save our way to wealth and that didn't happen. Then we moved to owning a business, or being self-employed, when we started the driving school. We slowly started seeing more money come in and we were no longer trading our time for a fixed amount of money. Our time was being traded for how much money we could earn.

We bring up opening your own business in this book because we want to share how we were able to leverage that $12,000 and turn it into $30,000 by the time we fixed our credit. We were able to get a nicer home just a short while later. By opening a business, we were able to save money faster than we would at a conventional job. In no way are we saying that having a regular job is bad – it's actually quite helpful in securing your loan. But if you want to pick up the pace where you can invest in more properties faster, owning a business can help speed that up.

So now you get to pick the pace you want to go. Do you like to move at a faster pace or do you like a slower pace? Neither is wrong and you absolutely get to choose. Just know that there is a cost to not taking action that you may want to also consider.

In the last 10 years, we've opened multiple business and here's what we learned about being successful:

1. Think Big, Start Small

You may have a huge vision about being financially free just like we did, but you have to fill a need in order to run a business that generates income. Keep your eye on that big vision for your goal, but start small. Ask yourself what people need right now. The more urgent their need, the faster they'll buy from your business.

2. Evaluate the Needs Gap

Just because you have a need, doesn't mean the market sees it the same. There are plenty of examples of failed business attempts shown on Shark Tank to illustrate exactly this. You might like the idea and you may need it in your life, but do other people feel the same? Research the need you're filling to make sure there's a big enough gap that people want it and then create a plan on how to fill it.

3. Model the Pros

If you can find others satisfying that same need and model the good things they're doing, you'll be well on your way to success with your new business. Even better, if you can find a mentor who is willing to help you, you can cut your learning curve. Plus a great mentor will save you from many costly mistakes.

4. Run a Phantom Ad

Test your theory. Place a phantom ad to make sure that you're filling that gap appropriately and you'll also create a lineup of people wanting what you have to offer before you're even open. You could book out your services two weeks down the road so you have enough time to get ready.

5. Start Before You're Ready

All our businesses, except the driving school, had a formal business plan. We thought we needed a business plan drawn up, website done, had decals for our car, created a budget, etc. We laugh about it now because we realized we didn't need all those things as much as we initially thought.

There's no need to over complicate it. All you need is to gather your research information and if it shows you can profitably fulfill a need, then execute! Your mind will start to play tricks on you about moving forward, but don't let it curtail your dreams. Trust us when we say that no one ever feels fully ready when they do new, exciting, and even scary things. However, successful people are able to see a great opportunity, ignore their own negative head chatter, and still move forward.

With each business, we've learned valuable lessons. And as we've generated more income and opened other businesses, we've let go of the ones that needed more time and focus. As we got busier, we favored the ones that needed less of our time and focus so that we could earn more money passively.

Top Mistakes to Avoid:

1. Using the "Follow Your Passion" Advice

Don't choose a business based on your passion. A lot of people on social media tout the "follow your passion and the money will follow" motto, but is that really true? If you really investigate, most people are not following their passion. They're in nine to five jobs and if they are going into business, they're usually not passionate about that business either. But eventually, when they've made enough money, they can divert money to their passion.

Please understand, we're not saying that following your passion never works. What we are saying is that you should evaluate your passion before you start because basing a decision on passion alone is not enough. We didn't start the driving school because of our passion; we didn't start the cleaning company because of our passion (we actually dislike cleaning). They were both created to meet a need.

The bottom line is that real estate will not be sustainable if you're not generating income no matter how passionate you are about it. It could cost you a lot of money and sleepless nights instead. The driving school and the cleaning business were a means to an end for us. At times you're in a job because you realize that you need to put food on the table for your family. It doesn't necessarily mean you're passionate about it, but you understand that it's a vehicle to get you where you're going. It's the same for any business you may open. There may be no passion attached to it, but you're doing what you need to in order to build that income so you could start working towards living your actual passion.

2. Over-Investing

Sometimes people can get zealous in setting up a new business. They rent a big, fancy office. They run out to get new clothes, over invest in marketing and promotional items, design a full website, etc. Then they also get stuck in the, "I need to do this before I can open," mentality and postpone their business launch. Some of these items are unnecessary to start.

When we started the driving school, we understood the business and the market. We knew how we were going to be different in the market. Our biggest purchase was the car and equipping it -- that was an absolute need. We also used a decal for the car that we took off when we used the car personally. We didn't even have an office because we didn't need it. For two years, we met people in coffee shops for sign ups in order to save money.

3. Holding Too Much Stock

Often if you have a product you're selling, you fall in love with it. You may get so excited that you buy too much of it. You may feel like you need to fully stock all the shelves or you want to send thousands of products to the Amazon warehouse in anticipation of your sales. Before you have your first customer, you've spent thousands of dollars without proof of concept. Sitting on idle inventory is a sure way to tie up money that could be used elsewhere.

What you may not be considering is that people get excited when things are sold out. You could start with 50 to 100 t-shirts or mugs and put "sold out" on the product when they're gone. Then create a waiting list knowing you've already sold much of your next bulk purchase. No more product stuck in your garage or basement collecting dust.

4. Getting High on Your Own Product

We've seen this happen especially with those involved in MLMs (Multilevel marketing). You become the biggest customer. You own every single product from the company you represent and every time something new comes out or there's a sale, you buy up a bunch of inventory to save for later. Sometimes people buy a lot of products just so that they can get to the top of the ranks in the company. You should only buy what you need.

5. The Boss-Only Mentality

We have seen people, even in immigrant communities, who don't want to get their hands dirty when starting a business. They feel proud to just be the boss and they want to immediately hire staff to oversee. You need to understand your business. You need to know the details of every position and be able to do each aspect, even as the boss. You probably have limited funds, so only hire people who are necessary in the beginning. Do some of the work yourself to start so you can save money until you can hire more staff. For example, instead of hiring five people right away, see if you could start with two or maybe just you. It may not be ideally what you want to do, but it will help you generate profits faster. Remember, it will be temporary.

It's funny how many of our businesses were created as we sat around the kitchen table brainstorming our next move. When we opened the cleaning (janitorial) business, it was just another business you might call an accident.

Colleen

I had been working at a small business who didn't appreciate my starting a business and working on it during lunch and after hours. I was fired and faced with a choice through unemployment to either get a regular job or open a business. Since the driving school was already operational, I had to come up with something else that wasn't in existence in order to qualify for the program. I looked to fill a need and our cleaning business was born.

When we think about real estate, it's just where we park our money. Any money we make from our other businesses get "parked" there. This was always the intention from the start. When you become more successful and you have excess money from other businesses, you'll need to decide what to do with it. We don't want to put the money in the bank because the interest is low. We would rather buy a bunch of residential or commercial properties because we know that we're winning in four ways: payments from tenants, passive appreciation, mortgage paydown, and active income.

One of our most recent sales was of a property we bought in 2016 for $320,000. When we bought it, we knew it was in a location that wouldn't appreciate in value but, we calculated that we would still come out ahead. We put $60,000 down and didn't improve the property in any way. We've sold it for the same amount, which isn't typical; however, we're received a $73,000 check because our tenants had been paying down the mortgage. We also received $600 a month in cash flow over the last four years equaling $7200 a year. Over four years, this is close to $30,000 on one property and a Cash on Cash return of about 17% per year. Where else can you get this kind of return on investment? This is exactly why we choose to park our money in real estate.

Chapter 18

Taking Massive Action

At this point, you've gotten a lot of information. We know how overwhelming it can feel and we congratulate you for getting this far in your real estate education. We're guessing you're really excited to embark on the journey to become financially free through real estate, but maybe you have doubts clouding your head. Know this is totally normal. Also know it doesn't need to feel that way. We've been able to get through obstacles, even the ones in our head, by knowing we have a proven strategy. You can use the same strategy we've used to amass millions in real estate. Our students have used the same strategy too. Your only job now is to take action and execute.

Some may even say it's a massive action that we've taken to realize and live our dream. A lot of people end up feeling confused or not sure what to do so we wanted to share eight steps that you can do to take massive action today too.

Step 1: Commit

The first step of taking massive action is knowing and committing to take action. Once you've set your mind in that zone, you'll be set up for success. There's a Chinese proverb that says, "The journey of 1000 miles begins with the first step." So the fact you have already taken the step to read this book is that initial step which is the most important step.

Step 2: Start Where You Are

What we mean by this is it's important to be realistic with your current situation because then you can decide where you want to go. We always talked to our clients about reverse engineering things. If you sit down and you think about where you want to be 20 years from now, you can figure out what you need to do to get there from where you are now. It all starts with where you are today.

Step 3: Take Small Steps

Let's say you want a yacht in 20 years. How do we get you there? It could be that you'll be 65 and that is the age when people are retiring. How are we going to get you that yacht? What are you doing to take those steps?

There's another saying that says, "Big dreams start with small steps." A lot of people have big dreams but they think it's not achievable because of money or maybe they see a big mountain to climb. It starts with the small steps. That's why declaring, "I want to be financially free," is an important step. Then figure what action steps you need to take to get there. When you make all those small steps a regular occurrence, they will add up and that's what will lead you to where you want to go.

Step 4: Mistakes are Learning Opportunities

Do not be afraid of restarting. Take your mess and let that become your message. All the mistakes we have made in the past are becoming the reason why we are the people we are today. We've learned from those experiences. Just think of all those stories we shared. In every single instance, we learned something new, applied it to the next purchase or tenant and got better. You can do the same.

Step 5: Keep Going No Matter What

"Our greatest glory is not in falling, it's in rising every time we fall." – Confucius

One of the biggest mistakes we made in our journey was believing a realtor who told us that purchasing a house with non-comforming suite was acceptable in our neighbourhood of choice. We bought a single family house with a basement and believed, without checking, that it was a conforming suite. That was one of the costliest mistakes we had made. If you remember, the neighbor got upset we were running an income property and called the city. The city wrote to us providing us with options to either resolve the situation or be forced to shut down. We had to re-invest money into legalizing the suite and lost cash flow as the tenant had to move out. Since we had taken the first steps of getting the property, we then had to take the next steps to rectify the issues.

The key message from that experience is to make sure you do your own due diligence. Do your own homework if you're committed to making this your business -- always verify the information that you've been provided.

Step 6: Always Be Learning

Every opportunity is one to learn. We remember when we started investing, we would designate time in our calendar to study concepts and strategies to invest in real estate. We were so focused as we knew we wanted to turn this into a business. After months of studying, we realized that we couldn't do it all and decided to find professionals who were experienced and could help us get to our goal. With each course, we executed and applied the new lessons we learned, and we were able to scale our business just by taking that step to learn.

Step 7: Be Patient with Results

As you probably have heard before, real estate is not a get rich quick scheme. From the amount of research on a quest to find the right deal, to the evaluations and calculations that need to be processed, to building a team, slow and steady wins the race. Reverse engineering your goals will help provide clarity on the end result, however, you must take the time to master your trade. Results may not appear in five or six years, sometimes even 10 years, but to see the fruits of your labor at the end will be worth it. It all depends on how you want to get educated to be able to get to where you need to be.

Chapter 19

FAQs about Real Estate Investing

Over the last few years, we've talked to new investors, been in real estate investment groups and been on countless interviews and over and over again the same questions pop up in regards to getting started and building a great portfolio. We're going to address these top questions here.

Question 1: How do you move from homeowner to investor?

That depends on your situation but let's address this in the most standard way:

1. Start by scheduling an appointment with your mortgage broker who will enlighten you on how much you can afford
2. Contact your accountant and discuss tax implications as they differ to your primary residence
3. A twenty percent down payment will be required for your purchase
4. Connect with your realtor to start the process of evaluating, eliminating, viewing and qualifying potential investment properties
5. Make an offer on the property, sign documents, provide deposit
6. Connect with lawyer
7. Conduct a property inspection

8. Offer accepted
9. Remove conditions
10. Advertise for tenants
11. Close on property and move in new tenants

There's nothing creative going on here so this is the standard "in the box" way to get your first property and become an investor.

As you can see, the process to becoming an investor on the property purchasing side is similar. The question we ask our students when they get started is, "Do you want to invest in real estate as a business or a hobby?". One owns a few cash flowing properties while the other is building an empire.

When taking the hobby approach, use the income suite method we've shared already to get your mortgage helper from that first property to pay down your mortgage. Then every two or three years, you can buy another property and repeat the same process until you have the number of properties that will give you the cash flow and appreciation you're looking for.

If you want to make real estate investing your business, you need to create a more structured plan and get educated in real estate investing which is something we do for our students every day. This strategy is different as a roadmap will have to be put together to execute your plan.

Question 2: Should you pay off your investment property?

Typically we advise against this strategy, but again, every person's situation is different. Generally if you are in growth mode, you want to refinance and reinvest as much as you can to grow your portfolio while letting the tenant pay off the original mortgage terms. This is a strategy to keep more liquid cash in your pockets to buy more properties. Please note this strategy does come with risks and must be carefully thought out and strategized.

For some people, paying off a property early is important for personal and business reasons. If your goal is to own your properties free and clear, we would recommend using an online software that can help you calculate what your mortgage loan would look like if you started paying more money each month towards the principal.

Question 3: What is a double offer?

A double offer strategy is where a buyer would put in one offer and then put in another competing offer at the same time. The sellers will know that both offers are coming from the buyer, but it's a way to get the seller to pick one of the two.

For example,
Offer #1: full price on a house at $350,000, close September 1st.
Offer #2: offer at $320,000, and close in two weeks on June 1st.

With this method, you're incentivizing the seller to accept an offer based on the closing date. If the seller isn't in a rush, they might take the full price deal and close September 1st. When the seller counters, you'll get a feel of where the seller is on timing and flexibility on price. Are they in a rush or are they okay to wait? Note that some realtors don't like this strategy.

Question 4: What is a red herring strategy?

The red herring strategy is where you use something as a distraction. Let's say your goal is to get this same $350,000 property for $320,000. Maybe the house is beautifully furnished, it's staged, and it has everything you want. You're going to use the furniture as a distraction so the sellers don't pay attention to the low price that is going to be on the offer. If the seller is attached to the furniture for any reason, they won't want to let it go. They're going to keep their focus on the distraction. They may wonder how you could even dare to offer $320,000 plus all their furniture. They'll put a price tag to the furniture.

You'll have to be okay with potentially offending the sellers with this because they'll feel like the furniture is worth a lot. Possibly outraged by your offer for the furniture, they've now become more willing to negotiate the price on the house. They might come back and say no to the furniture being included, but they'll now be willing to give you a discount on the purchase of the property. We've seen this also done with items like a riding lawn mower or a boat and most recently we made an offer on a property including a portable sauna.

Question 5: What is a Vendor Take Back?

A Vendor Take Back (VTB) also known as vendor financing is quickly becoming a strategy used amongst investors. It works like this: a buyer has identified a building for sale for seven hundred thousand dollars. The downpayment needed to complete this deal is $175,000 (25%). The buyer only has a downpayment of $125,000. They then approach the seller's agent and negotiate a VTB allowing them to be financed with the balance of $50,000 by the seller for an agreed upon time and interest rate. Right now they're in on the property for just $125,000 and can pay the seller the other $50,000 over the agreed upon time. The benefit to the seller is the buyer will be paying them interest on their loan.

If you run into this situation, the best thing to do is find out what the seller's motive for selling is. Maybe it's to buy a motorhome or maybe it's to go on vacation. It has to be a situation where the VTB would make sense and be beneficial to the seller. They are considered the vendor and they are financing the purchase of the property. You'll give them the down payment the same way you would with a bank except you're dealing with the seller. For added advantages, be sure to speak to your accountant if planning to use this strategy.

Question 6: What is seller financing?

Seller financing is typically carried out by homeowners or sellers who have paid off their property. This is a great opportunity for both parties. In this case, the seller becomes the bank. Where typically you would provide the bank with a downpayment, in this scenario a down payment would be provided to the seller via their lawyer . Many times in seller financing, sellers are motivated and you can negotiate better terms, including the interest rate, than what you would get at the bank. It could also be a strategy to use once you've exhausted all your bank financing options as you grow your real estate investment portfolio.

Question 8: How do you know the steps are the right steps?

First of all, know that you can't ever take all the right steps, but know that those steps will guide you to the things you need to do or know. So long as you're willing to learn, no step will be wasted. The biggest thing that will lead you to your success is knowing you are determined not to give up.

One of the pivotal moments for us was realizing we could either make all the mistakes that other investors had made and learn as we moved slowly or we could follow someone who was doing exactly what we wanted to do and we could start living the life we wanted sooner. By the time we realized we needed to get educated, we had already purchased two properties.

Did you know the average person who decides they want to be an investor on their own will buy one property every five years? We knew if our goal was to replace our income, one property every five years wouldn't cut it, especially once we had our son.

Zeb
Colleen was working for the government and was earning really good money. She had a pension and everything laid out for her, but her deep desire was to stay home with our son. Because we knew that, our focus was on properties that brought in the most revenue and that gave us enough cash flow to replace her income.

Question 9: Do You Recommend Investing Close to Home?

One of the reasons we chose to invest in the UK was to show our students the best investment was one that brought you closer to your goals regardless of location. In summary, you could pick a random country, travel there, start learning all you need to know about investing, buy a property and make money. We knew nothing about the UK, so we travelled there and spent a month conducting our research. Upon arrival, we dove straight into networking, attended training seminars and connected with realtors and wholesalers. We would joke and say that our flight was leaving at the end of the month but we weren't leaving without a property.

Due to our key connections, we purchased two properties that were both affordable and generated income. This ticked all the boxes we were looking for to prove you can invest anywhere, even outside of your home country.

When you're thinking about where you want to invest, it doesn't have to be that prime location everyone is talking about or is in a popular investment city. It just has to meet your goals.

When researching where to invest, one of the top things we look at when considering a market is the economy. It needs to be a diverse economy. There are markets around that could have high rents and good cash flow but because they are built on one economy when that one economy tanks, so does your investment.

So again, what is your strategy? Are you looking for a viable long term property? Are you in a good market for that? Opportunities are endless but it really comes down to what your strategy is?

Question 10: How Do You Qualify in Other Countries?

Ideally, you want to have your financing in place prior to visiting another country.

As the UK was our first international trip, we were not as prepared. When we decided we were going to invest in the UK, we checked with a few banks and none were able to finance us. Our trip forged ahead in hopes of working with B and C lenders but the interest rates were very high. We pivoted and partnered with a local investor whom we met while networking and purchased two properties together through joint ventures.

In the United States, we looked for US banks that would provide us with financing. This was a challenge. We managed to obtain a pre-approval from a local bank to purchase our Arizona properties. When considering investing in the States, the banks here in Canada will sometimes lend to Canadians buying US properties. As we were ready to place an offer, we discovered we needed special processing to complete our financing. We immediately contacted our realtor who connected us with a mortgage broker in the United States who could help foreign nationals like us.

It can be a challenge, but you will find your realtor is sometimes the best source for connecting with a mortgage broker. They have a vested interest in having you purchase a property and will likely connect you to mortgage brokers who can help you. Maximize and leverage your team's skill set. If they're commission based, they have a vested interest to help you get the deal done.

If you're planning on investing out of the country, have a good accountant on your team. They will guide you from a numbers and financial perspective on what the benefits of investing out of the country could be, especially from a tax perspective. They will also advise you if you should create a corporation or purchase under your personal names.

Our first two properties we bought in the States were purchased under our names. It obviously is a big risk considering that in the US, litigation is a big thing. But those properties, which are being used for short term rentals, have extremely good insurance coverage. We have put in place strategies that help with litigation. After that, we decided that they were going to officially be part of our business. They were not going to be one-off vacation homes that we could travel to, enjoy and rent out as an Airbnb.

We wanted to structure it accordingly because of that. That's when our accountant created a structure for us that made sense, understanding our goal from a Canadian perspective and also as a US investor.

For us, there hasn't been a set formula to find a place where we want to invest in properties. We didn't even know we were going to Phoenix until about a month before the trip. We are adventurers so we know if there's a place we enjoy travelling to repeatedly, we would rather have a place there that we use for Airbnb so that when we want to go there, we can block off the time and stay in our own investment property.

It's not out of the realm of possibilities for a friend or investor to say, "Hey, I've been looking at Mexico and I think you guys should check it out," and within two weeks to a month, we could be there to check out properties. We always run the numbers and get prepared before travelling so that we only go to locations where investing makes sense. We are a team of visionaries and action takers. We make it happen. It's a perfect Yin-Yang relationship.

Question 11: What Advice Would You Give Your Younger Self?

If we were to give our younger selves advice, it would be to make sure to understand credit and the power of surrounding yourself with people who push you. With the right influence, we could've started sooner if we had known. But instead, we delayed buying our first property because we just weren't eligible to buy anything.

Zeb

*It's amazing to control your own time. It's amazing not to
have to ask your boss for a vacation for your daughter's
sake or because you have to pick the kids up from
daycare. It's amazing to be in such a situation especially
for me because I was one of those people that most
people didn't think would achieve anything in life.*

And for those people who are on the journey, you don't
have to rush to quit your day job. It's an asset you have;
it's always harder as an investor to get a property without a
job. The second thing is 50 percent of a watermelon is
better than one hundred percent of a grape. A lot of people
would rather not joint venture because they want one
hundred percent of a grape. But what if you could get 50
percent of a watermelon while still working at your day
job? Shift the focus from, "I want to own all of these
properties," to, "I'm going to get a little bit of the pie
everywhere I go." You'll finally get to the point of replacing
your income so you can actually achieve your goals.

The bigger picture is, how do you move from 14 doors to
80 doors? How do you scale faster through joint ventures
or working with other people to reach your goals?

Chapter 20

What are some Common Deterrents and Mistakes in Real Estate Investing?

If you want to build wealth, including generational wealth, real estate investing is one of the best vehicles that can get you there. You may face some hiccups along the way dealing with tenants or other issues, but if you follow the strategies that we've shared, we know you can achieve it. They are the same strategies we've used for years and continue to teach our students who are gaining the financial freedom they once only dreamed of.

Through the years, we've come across many different properties, many different scenarios and helped countless people get started and grow their portfolios in real estate. Sometimes people get paralyzed trying to do everything perfectly. It's time to get comfortable with the idea you just don't know until you know. We can't go over every combination of situations that could occur because it would be endless, but we want to make sure you are aware of the most common misconceptions and mistakes that could deter you from real estate investment success.

1. It's a renter's market

You may have heard this before. People feel as if there are too many rentals out there. What if you're low balled on the amount of rent you advertised for? New investors get so wound up in this idea that they don't even start their real estate investing. How do you bust this belief? Don't focus on this being a renter's market. Put an ad out there to see if anyone's looking. You'll know if there is an actual need for your one or two bedroom basement suite. This is really part of doing your research before you make an offer on a property. There are so many cities out there so if one city doesn't seem like it's a market you want to invest in, move on to the next one.

2. What if I end up with bad tenants?

This is one of the biggest deterrents we've seen. People are so scared of bad tenants they drop the whole idea of building wealth this way. Some people may have heard from their friends who became accidental landlords that their experience was bad. Maybe they had to move because something in their life relocated them. They decided to rent out their home, without an exit strategy, without an investors' mindset, and without knowing how to be good property managers.

These accidental landlords just took the first renter that came to them without doing a credit check or getting other background information. Two or three months down the line, the tenants are not paying rent anymore or they've damaged the property. It spirals down from there as they share with all their friends and family to avoid real estate without taking basic investing knowledge.

3. What if the tenant doesn't pay rent?

Especially during stressful economic times, people worry about tenants not paying rent. Again, this is part of doing your due diligence. Check the vacancy rates. Check the unemployment rates. See what the outlook for the city is. Credit check your tenants and check their references. We can't predict everything, but knowing the demographics of a city can help you avoid these types of problems as much as possible.

4. Real Estate Isn't Liquid

Some people say they don't want to tie up their money in real estate. They express how they would rather put their money in a savings account and be able to access it whenever they want. What we tell our students is you can get a mortgage and have an option, like a line of credit, where you can take out money at any time. Your money can be liquid if you set it up to be that way all while investing in real estate.

5. Lending Requirements are Too Tough

We all know the bank is really tightening their wallet and their conditions right now. They're not lending as much as they were in the past.

If we rewind back to when we started our journey a few years ago, we were not getting all the perks that people who invested in 2008 received. The rules changed but that didn't stop us from moving forward just because we weren't allowed to assume mortgages anymore. Instead, we decided to take the situation for what it was in 2014 regardless of how hard things had become. The interest rates were higher than they are now. So why not look at the positive side of what's going on? You can qualify for more of a house with lower interest rates.

6. The Real Estate Market is not Low Enough Now

At the time of writing this book, we are in the midst of the COVID-19 pandemic. The newspapers and the news on TV are talking about how the prices are going to plummet due to the pandemic. Some people have decided to use this as an excuse to postpone buying properties. They think waiting is a better idea. What if you could negotiate terms and prices that worked regardless of which direction the markets went? Don't wait to invest, invest in real estate then wait.

Let's switch gears and talk about the stock market. Remember when it hit a bottom? There were plenty of people who were waiting for that "perfect" rock bottom time and then they completely missed a great deal entirely. You can never time the market perfectly. None of us have a crystal ball, but if you're going to invest in real estate, you need to do it for the long term.

If your strategy is to buy and hold, getting the exact bottom number isn't as important as it is to find the right property in the right area. Real estate is not a get rich quick scheme. Along the way, your house value may go up, but it also may come down. If you've done the calculations like we've taught you and you're playing the long game, you have enough of a cushion to know that in the event this happens, you won't lose if you can hold on until the market goes back up.

7. There Aren't Any Good Homes Close to Me

It's important when looking for a rental property to talk to your realtor about the locations you're interested in. They are a part of your team and have expertise you may not have like which locations are better to invest in. With the right team, you will get a property in the right location and you will get good tenants.

Remember that just because other people, including perhaps friends and family, have tried real estate investing before without success, it doesn't mean you are also going to have the same experience. Be sure you actually seek help in advance and get advice from professionals that will make great team members.

Do not buy into a market on speculation. You can easily misjudge the resale or rental value. If you think a home is a good deal at $350,000 because the other houses are around $500,000, make sure you're doing your research to find out why that specific house is a certain amount. You might find that there are issues with the house, like a bad foundation or an infestation. Maybe it only has three bedrooms and one bath instead of three bedrooms, two baths. Maybe that house doesn't have a basement, it's missing a garage or maybe the square footage is smaller.

The Top Three Real Estate Investing Mistakes

One of our goals with writing this book is to share the truth of what it really takes to be a successful real estate investor. Our journey has truly transformed our lives and we know that what we get to pass on to future generations is invaluable. No longer will our children or our children's children be bound by the plans society has for them. They will understand they can passively make income with real estate and they'll know financial freedom isn't just for those born into affluence. Anyone can do this if they want it badly enough.

While we have mentioned these mistakes throughout the book, we want to highlight them again now because it's important to know what keeps people from success in real estate.

1. Not Doing the Calculations

Use our guidance with the calculations so you know right away how much cash flow you'll be making. Too many people try to skip this step, estimate, or do complicated calculations in their heads and this is where they lose. To help you with mortgage calculations, one of our favorite mortgage calculator apps is "Canadian Mortgage App".

2. Letting Your Emotions Drive Your Decisions

Remember to purchase based on the facts, not emotions or the pure excitement of buying your next property. This is a big one. When you walk into a house and you really like all the staging and the millions of other reasons why this house is perfect for you, don't let your emotions cloud your judgment. Do your numbers to avoid overpaying for properties. Staged homes always have glitz and glam to entice you to pay $10,000 more for the property. When you sit down and do the numbers, you'll realize it's actually not worth that much. You will be a better real estate investor by running the numbers rather than falling in love with places that "feel like home." Besides, you're not the one who's living there.

3. No Exit Strategy

Know how you will exit the property when you buy it. What happens when you decide to sell the property? Most of the time when we buy a property to live in, we never plan on leaving. But that doesn't stop us from having an exit strategy just in case. Life happens and you need to have a plan when you decide to leave. Do I exit by selling as it's in a good location that's going up in value? Can I rent it out? What are my other options?

You will want to consider these and other questions. Who's going to buy the property? For example, if you have a single family home, or even a duplex or triplex, you have a bigger market than someone who has a 30 unit apartment building. Someone who invests in a 30 unit apartment building already knows when it's time to sell in 25 years or so, there's a limited number of people who will be interested. Those people are strictly investors. On the other hand, if you have a duplex or a single family home, you have a wider market and a bigger pool of people who will be interested in your property.

Even though we called this chapter the deterrents and mistakes in real estate investing, they don't have to be things that hold you back. For every issue, problem or fear you may have in starting or continuing your journey, there is a solution. At times, it may not seem like there is a solution, so you may have to get creative, do something you don't look forward to doing, undertake something that's never been done before, or consult with someone further ahead than you are. The key here is to keep your eye on the vision for your financial freedom and work through anything that comes up.

Chapter 21

Conclusion

Real estate investing is not just about learning the steps, doing calculations, buying properties and following the "rules". It's about a lifestyle and a vision that gives you and your family financial freedom, even if you're a new immigrant. We went into investing wide-eyed, with big dreams and some days it felt like we were being told to throw in the towel. Instead, we took those obstacles and turned them into lessons and realized that The Universe wasn't telling us to give up – it was asking us how badly we wanted it.

Now we are international investors. If you had asked us ten years ago if this is what we had in mind, we would tell you what we've created is well beyond our wildest dreams.

Zeb

There was time that we lost the vision for real estate. I remember how I felt telling Colleen I was going to drop out of University. I was scared of what she might say and I thought she might reject the idea, or even reject me. I wasn't sure if she would think dropping out of school was a good idea, but through it all, we've been so blessed to have each other. Where my weaknesses lie, Colleen has her strengths and we complement each other so well in business and life.

There are so many more topics we could discuss like wholesaling, section 8 housing, REITs, commercial property, etc. but that would make this book overwhelming. And we know when people feel overwhelmed, they don't execute and if they never execute, they'll never even get their first property.

There's nothing worse than rolling through life in the passenger's seat. You're at the mercy of other people and they're dictating what you can and can't do. You drift through every day hoping that something will happen, you'll get a lucky break or you'll get inspired to go a different direction. But it doesn't happen.

Here's what we know: you get to make your own destiny. You can create your own type of "luck" and you can stop sitting around at home, binge watching Netflix, staying up late eating ice cream only to repeat the same day every day. Isn't it time to stop living your version of Groundhog Day?

Buy your first mortgage helper property and invest in more real estate because your confidence to become financially literate won't fall on your lap. Confidence is created when you execute and as you execute more, it becomes more familiar and easy. Then your confidence grows. But waiting for confidence to fall out of the sky won't happen.

Don't you want your weekdays back? Don't you want your weekends to have meaning? What if you could get up and travel wherever you wanted whenever you want or just take in a movie in the middle of the day with your family?

And if you join our group,16WeekInvestor here: https://www.facebook.com/groups/16weekinvestor/, you'll not only be able to connect personally with us, but also find a variety of people who can keep you encouraged and accountable along the way.

We know what can happen now that you've finished reading the book. You could start doubting yourself and think, "That was nice." You may think you need to be "special" in some way. Perhaps you wonder, "Who do I think I am?" and you beat yourself up about all the things in your past that didn't work out the way you wanted. But this is your time to choose – you get to choose the outcome you want and you can choose to be different this time around. If you were someone who didn't feel capable or smart enough in the past, or you failed to complete projects before, you get to draw a line in the sand and promise to show up differently for this because it means something to you.

Colleen
I remember a time I thought life was good enough. I had quit my job and we had good cash flow on our investments. Did we really need to buy more properties? Couldn't we just be done and continue to travel and have fun in life? But something inside me knew there was more for us. This wasn't the end of our real estate investing. We wanted to make sure we had a portfolio that would help our children, our grandchildren and maybe even our great grandchildren and beyond. We wanted apartment buildings where our kids could say, "My parents own that" And we could teach them to teach future generations to stay out of the rat race.

See, the root of any problem in life or business is in your own head. You just need to decide to take matters into your own hands, get educated, and determine that you cannot fail. What would happen if you told yourself that it was impossible not to hit your goals? How would you feel? What would you do? How excited would you be?

We were and are just like you. The only difference you might see is that we are stubborn and persistent. We worked through every issue and we didn't take failure as an option. In the last ten years, we have gone through the rollercoaster of learning and figured out how to master real estate investing, both from a practical perspective and a mental toughness perspective. That's why we made sure this book gave you the real truth of what it looks like to get into real estate and deal with tenants.

Here's what it takes in a nutshell:
- Confidence
- Perseverance
- Lifelong Learning
- Belief in Yourself
- Breaking the Molds
- Great Attitude
- Endurance
- Creativity
- Ability to Delegate
- Willingness to Win
- Seeing Setbacks and Lessons

The great thing is that these are skills you can develop if you choose to commit to the vision of becoming financially free and follow through to execute on what we teach you. What we share will seep into other aspects of your life – your relationship and your health even. You'll feel more compelled to be excellent at all of it.

Just think about how that, in and of itself, will change your life. You'll be happier, more fulfilled, purpose-filled, mission-driven and you'll be a legacy builder for your family. You may accomplish things no one in your family has ever done. You may break a cycle of under-earning and settling in your lineage.

That's why it's so important right now you don't say, *"I'll start next week after (insert event or excuse here)"*

That thought alone is 100% proof you need to start right away.

We can promise you what you will gain in following our strategies will far outweigh any and all reasons to wait to start. The process is simple; we lay it out step-by-step in our programs. But you have to be willing to follow through with zero compromises and don't skip steps just because you don't like them or they make you feel uncomfortable.

You can do this no matter what your starting point is. You may have bad credit and zero savings or you might have already purchased a property but you don't know how to grow your future portfolio correctly. Either way, now is the time to stop talking about all the things that you want in life and start taking the steps to make real advancements towards them.

Life is about choices. You can go down the road you're already on and muddle through life wondering what would've happened if you had followed our advice, joined our group and gotten the coaching that we offer. Or you could jump in like we did, trusting that we were hiring the right mentors to get us to exactly where we wanted to be. We definitely aren't done yet with our real estate investing. So much opens up for us every time we talk with other investors and we keep our eyes open for opportunities. And now we invite you to join us on the journey.

About Us

Colleen Tsikira wears a number of professional hats. She identifies as a serial entrepreneur with business interests spanning across real estate investing, start-up business investing, and property management. She is the co-owner of several business ventures.

Colleen strongly believes in utilizing the reach of our standing as professionals in developing communities and she's a community advocate in that regard. Her career path has defined her passion for mentorship in entrepreneurship as well. After graduating in Business Administration in 2010 and researching various business models, Colleen branched into real estate investment. An ability and talent to spot opportunities paired with her ambition allowed Colleen to triple her business to over 6 figures in less than a year. She managed to build a Multi-million Dollar Real Estate portfolio in her mid-20's and doubled clients' profits in her coaching business.

In this present day, her business has been a roaring success that has allowed her to travel the world and explore new investment opportunities and markets. The progression of Colleen's story, which stems from childhood entrepreneurial tendencies has motivated her to start an investor mentorship program with her husband. This has also resulted in her doing volunteer community work.

Zeb Tsikira is a serial entrepreneur with a vast portfolio in real estate that cuts into international markets from his base in Canada. He has start-up entrepreneurial experience that spans over a decade and has a passion for mentorship and creating generational wealth.

Together with his wife, Zeb has created an investor platform whose main aim is to educate and train people on financial intelligence with particular emphasis on real estate and property management.

An inspirational figure, mentor and icon in his trade, Zeb dropped out of university to chase his dream and defy the odds by registering viable projects that have turned their business into a multi-million dollar investment. He currently travels around the world on various mentorship and business assignments. Starting out as an immigrant and working his way up whilst studying, Zeb epitomizes the ultimate against all odds story.

He is passionate about community causes and sponsors university students in Zimbabwe as well as engaging with various community organizations to champion empowerment.

References

(1) Urosevic, Milan. (2020, November 11). 21+ American Savings Statistics to Know in June 2020 [blog post]. Retrieved from https://spendmenot.com/blog/american-savings-statistics/

(2) Dimbuene, Zacharie Tsala & Turcotte, Martin. (2020, November 11). Study on International Money Transfers from Canada [blog post]. Retrieved from https://www150.statcan.gc.ca/n1/pub/89-657-x/89-657-x2019007-eng.htm

(3) Kagan, Julia. (2020, November 11). Universal Life (UL) Insurance [blog post]. Retrieved from https://www.investopedia.com/terms/u/universallife.asp

(4) Parker, Tim. (2020, November 11). The Value of Universal Life by Retirement [blog post]. Retrieved from https://www.investopedia.com/articles/personal-finance/020916/universal-life-how-much-cash-value-retirement.asp

(5) Forbes Wealth. (2020, November 11). Canadians Lack Personal Savings [blog post]. Retrieved from https://forbeswealthblog.ca/2019/09/canadians-lack-personal-savings/

(6) Dhillon, Laddi. (2020, November 11). The Lifetime of a House [blog post]. Retrieved from http://www.houseinbrampton.ca/b/blog/the-lifetime-of-a-house.html

Made in USA - Kendallville, IN
21708_9781777385125
03.04.2022 1452